History of Ancient Mexico

An Enthralling Guide to Pre-Columbian Mexico and Its Civilizations, Such as the Olmecs, Maya, Zapotecs, Mixtecs, Toltecs, and Aztecs

© Copyright 2023 - All rights reserved.

The content contained within this book may not be reproduced, duplicated, or transmitted without direct written permission from the author or the publisher.

Under no circumstances will any blame or legal responsibility be held against the publisher, or author, for any damages, reparation, or monetary loss due to the information contained within this book, either directly or indirectly.

Legal Notice:

This book is copyright protected. It is only for personal use. You cannot amend, distribute, sell, use, quote, or paraphrase any part, or the content within this book, without the consent of the author or publisher.

Disclaimer Notice:

Please note the information contained within this document is for educational and entertainment purposes only. All effort has been executed to present accurate, up-to-date, reliable, and complete information. No warranties of any kind are declared or implied. Readers acknowledge that the author is not engaging in the rendering of legal, financial, medical, or professional advice. The content within this book has been derived from various sources. Please consult a licensed professional before attempting any techniques outlined in this book.

By reading this document, the reader agrees that under no circumstances is the author responsible for any losses, direct or indirect, that are incurred as a result of the use of the information contained within this document, including, but not limited to, errors, omissions, or inaccuracies.

Free limited time bonus

Stop for a moment. We have a free bonus set up for you. The problem is this: we forget 90% of everything that we read after 7 days. Crazy fact, right? Here's the solution: we've created a printable, 1-page pdf summary for this book that you're reading now. All you have to do to get your free pdf summary is to go to the following website:

https://livetolearn.lpages.co/enthrallinghistory/

Once you do, it will be intuitive. Enjoy, and thank you!

Table of Contents

INTRODUCTION 1
PART ONE: KEY CIVILIZATIONS 3
   CHAPTER 1: THE OLMECS 4
   CHAPTER 2: THE MAYA 12
   CHAPTER 3: THE ZAPOTECS 22
   CHAPTER 4: THE MIXTECS 30
   CHAPTER 5: THE TOLTECS... 37
   CHAPTER 6: THE AZTECS 46
PART TWO: HISTORICAL PERIODS.. 55
   CHAPTER 7: PRECLASSIC MEXICO (1900 BCE-250 CE) 56
   CHAPTER 8: MEXICO IN THE CLASSIC PERIOD (250-900 CE) .. 65
   CHAPTER 9: POSTCLASSIC MEXICO (900-1521 CE)................ 73
PART THREE: THE FIGHT FOR ANCIENT MEXICO........................... 80
   CHAPTER 10: PREPARING FOR BATTLE 81
   CHAPTER 11: THE SPANISH CONQUEST AND ITS AFTERMATH 89
PART FOUR: AN UNFORGETTABLE LEGACY 99
   CHAPTER 12: LEGENDARY FIGURES 100
   CHAPTER 13: ART, ARCHITECTURE, AND ARTIFACTS........................ 109
   CHAPTER 14: ANCIENT CITIES.. 120
   CHAPTER 15: ANCIENT MYTHOLOGY AND COSMOLOGY 128
   CHAPTER 16: ANCIENT MEXICAN CULTURE AND LEGACY 136
CONCLUSION 144
HERE'S ANOTHER BOOK BY ENTHRALLING HISTORY THAT YOU MIGHT LIKE.. 147
FREE LIMITED TIME BONUS... 148
BIBLIOGRAPHY 149

Introduction

On the Lake of the Moon sat the idyllic island city of Aztlán, where elegant white herons stood regally among the reeds. The lake teemed with large fish, ducks paddled in the shallows, and brilliant yellow and red songbirds flitted among the trees. In the middle of this picturesque island rose a high hill, and under its craggy slopes were seven caves. Seven tribes emerged from these seven caves, according to the Mexica genesis myths. Collectively called the Aztecs for their island of origin, the seven tribes left the island one by one. The last to go was the Mexica, around nine centuries ago.

Why did they leave their island of abundance? This part of the story is unclear; perhaps some traumatic event happened, such as an invasion or an earthquake. But their comfortable life abruptly ended when they started to wander through Mexico's northwestern desert in "a land turned against them." Jagged rocks, cacti, and thistles tore at their feet as they dodged slithering rattlesnakes and venomous Gila monsters. The Mexica finally emerged in the Valley of Mexico, the highlands plateau in central Mexico encompassing today's Mexico City, where their six kinsmen tribes had already settled.[1]

For thousands of years before the seven Aztec tribes arrived in central Mexico, other fascinating civilizations ruled central and southern Mexico. The Olmecs erected pyramids and palaces on the Gulf Coast beginning

---

[1] Wayne Elzey, "A Hill on a Land Surrounded by Water: An Aztec Story of Origin and Destiny," *History of Religions,* 31, no. 2 (1991):105-49. http://www.jstor.org/stable/1063021.

around 1600 BCE. Later, the Teotihuacanos built the largest city in the Americas in the Valley of Mexico's northeastern corner. Although they are crumbling today, the majestic ruins stand as an astonishing testament to the two advanced civilizations that existed when the Mexica arrived.

The Maya, contemporaries of the Olmec, built their spectacular cities in the jungles and highlands of the Yucatán Peninsula, southern Mexico, and Central America. The artistic Zapotecs and Mixtecs arose in the later days of the Olmec, thriving in the Puebla and Oaxaca regions of southern Mexico, stretching to the Pacific coast. The mighty Toltecs arrived in central Mexico about the time of Teotihuacan's fall, but their grand civilization imploded before the Aztecs arrived.

This book explores the interrelated stories of the remarkable civilizations that left an indelible mark on Mexico's history. We will unwrap the tales of their legendary figures, examine the art and architecture of these magnificent cultures, and learn about their epic wars, mythology, and religious practices. Finally, we will discuss what happened when Spanish ships arrived on Mexico's shores in the early sixteenth century.

Learning history has multiple benefits. It helps us understand why things are the way they are today. We capture valuable knowledge we can apply to modern-day scenarios from the phenomenal victories and dismal failures of the past. While some of Mexico's ancient cultures stand in stark contrast to today's Mexico, some things haven't changed much at all. Let's explore the magical mysteries of ancient Mexico and uncover a legacy that continues to impact our world today.

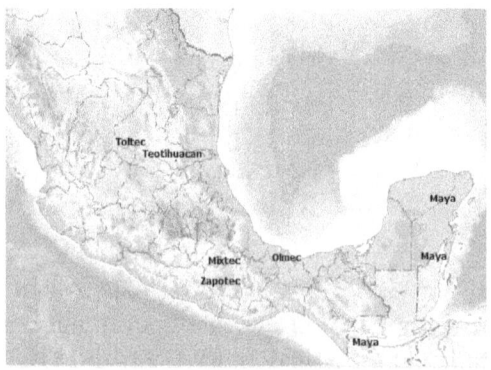

Pre-Aztec civilizations in Mexico.
Photo modified: zoomed in, labels added. Credit: Addicted04, CC BY-SA 3.0 <https://creativecommons.org/licenses/by-sa/3.0>, via Wikimedia Commons; https://commons.wikimedia.org/wiki/File:Mexico_topographic_map-blank_2.svg

PART ONE:
Key Civilizations

Chapter 1: The Olmecs

Chocolate, colossal heads, and rubber balls: the Olmecs invented them all! They also built the first known pyramid in North America. As the "mother culture" of Mesoamerica (the region from central Mexico to Costa Rica), the Olmec culture evolved into a higher civilization without any known outside influence. Their cultural prototypes, which later Mesoamerican civilizations copied, included pyramids, glyph-writing, and aligning their cities according to their 260-day religious calendar.[2]

The Olmec civilization emerged in the marshy, warm region near the Gulf of Mexico, today's Veracruz and Tabasco. Around 8000 BCE, the beginning of the Mesoamerican Archaic period, hunters and gatherers began segueing into a more sedentary agricultural lifestyle. Corn became the staple crop in the farm villages of the pre-Olmec around 2500 BCE. The Olmecs morphed from primitive farmers into Mesoamerica's first complex civilization around 1800 BCE, near the beginning of Mesoamerica's Preclassic period. The Olmecs introduced North America to its first cities, pyramids, calendar, writing system, and aqueducts.

We have no idea what the Olmecs called themselves, but in the Nahuatl language of the Aztecs, "Olmec" meant "rubber people." The Olmecs discovered that if they mixed sap from rubber trees with sap from morning glory vines, the resulting goo was pliable enough to wrap around

---

[2] Ronald A. Grennes-Ravitz and G. H. Coleman, "The Quintessential Role of Olmec in the Central Highlands of Mexico: A Refutation," *American Antiquity* 41, no. 2 (1976): 196. https://doi.org/10.2307/279172.

rocks. Rubber has many practical uses, but for the Olmecs, the main point of inventing rubber was for bouncy balls.[3]

The Olmecs played a ball game with these rubber balls. The game consisted of two teams in a sunken courtyard with a goal on each end. In this soccer-like game, which the Aztecs later called ulama, the players hit the ball with their hips, forearms, and heads to move it to their goal. The game became an intrinsic part of Mesoamerican culture and was connected to religious festivities. Almost two thousand ancient ballcourts have been unearthed In Mexico and Central America. Villagers in Sinaloa, Mexico, still play a version of ulama today.

Olmec heartland.
Original Version author Madman2001, edited version author:RG, CC BY 3.0
<https://creativecommons.org/licenses/by/3.0>, via Wikimedia Commons;
https://commons.wikimedia.org/wiki/File:800px-Olmec_Heartland_Overview_5.jpg

The Olmec's earliest known ceremonial center was El Manatí, built around 1700 BCE at the foot of Cerro Manatí (Manatee Hill) in the swampy floodplains of the Coatzacoalcos River. And, yes, they already had rubber balls. Archaeologists found twelve balls, thirty-seven carved

---

[3] Dorothy Hosler, et al., "Prehistoric Polymers: Rubber Processing in Ancient Mesoamerica," *Science*, June 18, 1999, 1988-91. doi:10.1126/science.284.5422.1988. OCLC 207960606. PMID 10373117.

wooden human busts, jade axe heads, and the skeletons of newborn babies, possibly human sacrifices.

The early Olmecs were drinking chocolate about 3,700 years ago. Researchers tested residue at the bottom of a ceramic vessel in El Manatí and found theobromine, an alkaloid chemical in the cacao plant. Later, archaeologists uncovered over twenty cups with chocolate residue at the Olmec site of San Lorenzo. The ingenious Olmecs had figured out how to ferment and roast cacao beans to make a chocolate drink.[4]

When the Olmecs weren't playing ball or drinking chocolate, they were hard at work building cities. After settling along the Coatzacoalcos River around 1450 BCE, the Olmecs hauled tons of dirt in baskets to construct a 140-acre plateau with terraces descending to the wetlands. They built their first small city, known today as San Lorenzo, around 1200 BCE on this plateau on the banks of the Coatzacoalcos River in southeast Veracruz. San Lorenzo was a religious and trade center with a population of about five thousand, although it served around thirteen thousand people in the surrounding farming communities covering thirty square miles. Two other Olmec towns stood next to the river to the north and south of San Lorenzo.

Another Olmec pioneering marvel was a complex aqueduct system with underground pipes moving fresh spring water into San Lorenzo. The Western Hemisphere's first known conduit drainage system featured 300 tons of U-shaped basalt troughs with removable covers traveling over a 550-foot mainline. It emptied into a duck-shaped cistern that had the carving of a duck on it.[5]

A hallmark of Olmec culture was its colossal heads, which were about ten feet high and weighed around eight tons. The Olmecs carved them from basalt, a rock formed by rapidly cooling lava, from the Cerro Cintepec and San Martín volcanoes of the Tuxtlas Mountains. Cerro Cintepec was sixty miles north of San Lorenzo, and the San Martín volcano was almost one hundred miles away. How the Olmecs transported these eight-ton sculptures over that distance without the wheel or beasts of burden is mind-boggling. Were they dragged over land or moved by raft on the river system? Either transport method was a jaw-

---

[4] T. G. Powis, et al., "Cacao Use and the San Lorenzo Olmec," *Proceedings of the National Academy of Sciences*, 108(21) (2011): 8595-600.

[5] Alison Bailey Kennedy, "Ecce Bufo: The Toad in Nature and in Olmec Iconography," *Current Anthropology* 23, no. 3 (1982): 286-7. http://www.jstor.org/stable/2742313.

dropping engineering feat requiring tremendous manpower.

An Olmec colossal head with a helmet.
TomClark18, CC BY-SA 4.0 <https://creativecommons.org/licenses/by-sa/4.0>, via Wikimedia Commons; https://commons.wikimedia.org/wiki/File:Olmec_colossal_head_5_.gif

The faces of the colossal heads are distinctive. The colossal heads probably represent a real person, such as a king. They wear helmets, suggesting they might have been warriors or ball players. Their almond-shaped eyes, broad noses, and full lips seem Polynesian or even African. However, the mitochondrial DNA of two Olmec skeletons dating from 1200 and 1000 BCE found they belong to haplogroup A, the indigenous American population. The Olmecs painted these carvings with bright colors, although that has worn off over the past three millennia. Ten of these enormous carvings were in San Lorenzo, although there were several in other Olmec cities.

The Olmecs' primary food was maize (corn), but they also consumed avocado, beans, chocolate, squash, and sweet potato. They raised dogs for food, hunted white-tailed deer and peccaries, and harvested fish from the river. Their extensive trade network used the river system and penetrated four hundred miles northwest into the Basin of Mexico and five hundred miles southeast into Guatemala. They traded rubber, figurines, and ceramics for jade, colorful feathers, and the razor-sharp volcanic obsidian they used for knives and spearheads.

San Lorenzo had elite residences at the highest point of its artificial plateau. Its palatial structures included the "red palace," which featured basalt columns supporting the roof and a basalt drain. Red ochre (iron oxide mixed with clay) covered the plastered walls and floors. Next to the red palace were a basalt workshop and another workshop that recycled older sculptures by carving fresh faces on them. Non-elite residents lived in wattle and daub homes on the city's lower terraces. These houses had a wooden lattice framework covered with a mixture of clay and straw.

San Lorenzo declined, with its population dispersing, around 850 BCE, probably due to the river changing course. Meanwhile, a new Olmec city sprang up on an island on a Tonalá River tributary ten miles from the Gulf of Mexico. La Venta, the new Olmec capital, was considerably larger, with an estimated population of twenty thousand. The Stirling Acropolis was a temple complex adjacent to a ballcourt and the Great Pyramid.

La Venta's pyramid and other significant structures are aligned eight degrees west of north. Some other major Mesoamerican cities, like Teotihuacan, had an astronomical northern alignment. This alignment is probably related to where the sun rose at the beginning and end of their 260-day ritual year, which fit into their 365-day solar year (they had both). Scholars believe the 260-day calendar used throughout Mesoamerica began with the Olmecs at La Venta around 800 BCE but was possibly used earlier in San Lorenzo. Using lidar imaging technology, researchers recently found hundreds of ancient Mesoamerican cities aligned with the 260-day calendar. This new study supports the hypothesis that the Olmecs initially developed the Mesoamerican calendar system and the astronomically-oriented alignment of cities.[6]

What appears to be a hill rising over a plateau is actually the remains of La Venta's Great Pyramid, the first in Mesoamerica. Erected in the core of the city's ceremonial center, it stands over one hundred feet high. The tallest manmade structure in Mesoamerica at that time, it was built of packed clay, and stepped sides covered with stone slabs rose from its rectangular base. Eight stelae (stone pillars or slabs) stood in a row on the southern side of the pyramid, facing away from it.

---

[6] Ivan Sprajc, et al., "Origins of Mesoamerican Astronomy and Calendar: Evidence from the Olmec and Maya Regions," *Science Advances* 9, no. 1 (2023). doi:10.1126/sciadv.abq7675.

Great Pyramid of La Venta.
Photo modified: zoomed in.
https://commons.wikimedia.org/wiki/File:La_Venta_Pir%C3%A1mide_cara_norte.jpg

Tres Zapotes was another significant Olmec city about sixty miles west of La Venta. Built around 1000 BCE, it encompassed about two hundred acres but did not display the ostentatious wealth of La Venta. In 1862, a farmer's hoe clanked on something, which turned out to be a colossal head, and that's how Tres Zapotes was discovered. Unlike San Lorenzo and La Venta, which each had an extravagant central administrative and religious complex, Tres Zapotes had four plazas about one-half mile apart. Each plaza was built around 400 BCE with a pyramid on its west side and a similar platform arrangement.

The Olmecs developed the first writing system in North America: a primitive form of hieroglyphics. The Cascajal Block is a foot-long serpentine stone with sixty-two symbols running horizontally. Some glyphs appear to depict corn, fish, insects, and pineapple; others are more abstract. Road builders discovered the stone in the late 1990s in a pile of debris close to ancient San Lorenzo, and scholars dated it to the late 900s BCE. In 1997 and 1998, another stone and a cylinder seal were discovered only three miles from La Venta, with glyphs dating to around 650 BCE.

Like San Lorenzo, La Venta experienced an abrupt depopulation around 400 BCE. This time, the city and the entire eastern Olmec heartland lost their population, leaving the region almost empty for two millennia. Only Tres Zapotes, one hundred miles west of La Venta, survived. Tens of thousands of Olmecs suddenly died or vacated the eastern area. What happened? Apparently, a horrific environmental catastrophe thrust the culture into extinction.

What sort of apocalyptic disaster could do this? Three enormous tectonic plates lie under Mexico, and earthquakes and volcanoes result when they shift and upheave. Mexico ranks number nine worldwide for volcanoes in the Holocene epoch (going back almost twelve thousand years). The El Chichón volcano is about sixty miles from La Venta and is still active, erupting last in 1981. It is part of the Chiapanecan Volcanic Arc, where three great tectonic plates collide: the North American Plate, the Caribbean Plate, and the Cocos Plate.

Mexico experiences thousands of earthquakes annually and averages about one earthquake a year that is greater than a 6.1 magnitude. The Olmec territory was slightly out of the most active earthquake range, yet with its soft, marshy soil, even mild tremors could have damaged buildings. Tectonic shifting could also have generated volcanic activity and changes in the river system on which the Olmecs depended.

An insidious aspect of active volcanoes is carbon dioxide in the plumes and fumaroles. Carbon dioxide is heavier than air and can collect in low-lying areas, such as the Olmec marshy heartland. Air with over 3 percent carbon dioxide causes dizziness, headaches, and trouble breathing. If it reaches 15 percent, this lethal gas will kill all human, animal, and plant life. Carbon dioxide could have suddenly and silently wiped out life in the low-lying areas of the Olmec territory.

Although what happened to La Venta and the eastern Olmec heartland is unclear, an exodus of survivors moved to Tres Zapotes in the west. This was when the Tres Zapotes residents built the four similar ceremonial plazas at equal distances from each other, hinting at a co-ruling situation or a more egalitarian society. Some eastern Olmecs also flooded into the Olmec town of Cerro de las Mesas, northwest of Tres Zapotes.

A new culture called the Epi-Olmec, apparently an extension of the Olmec civilization, flourished in Tres Zapotes and Cerro de las Mesas until around 250 CE. Tres Zapotes persisted for two thousand years through the Olmec, Epi-Olmec, and Classic Veracruz civilizations. The Epi-Olmecs did not display the flamboyant wealth of La Venta and San Lorenzo, and they didn't import luxury goods from afar. The Olmec trade empire collapsed, and most of what the Epi-Olmecs had was locally produced.

Although the Epi-Olmec didn't have the lavish Olmec lifestyle, they still made cultural strides. They used the Long Count calendar, which kept track of the years going back to their perceived date of the creation of humans: 3114 BCE. Interestingly, that date was close to when the pre-Olmecs began settling the Veracruz and Tabasco areas and engaging in more formal agriculture. Although the Olmecs had simple hieroglyphics, the Epi-Olmec developed the more sophisticated Isthmian hieroglyphic script. A farmer in the Tuxtlas mountain region unearthed the Tuxtla Statuette: a half-man and half-duck creature. Seventy-five glyphs were carved into the figurine with a date from the Long Count calendar (162 CE in our calendar).

In 1939, part of a rectangular stone block called Stela C was unearthed in Tres Zapotes, and thirty years later, the rest of it was discovered. Stela C had Isthmian script on one side and a Long Count calendar date corresponding to 32 BCE. In 1986, anthropologists were thrilled when the four-ton La Mojarra Stela was found in the Acula River, close to Tres Zapotes. It had a portrait of an elaborately costumed man etched in part of the stone, and 535 glyphs and 2 dates, corresponding to 143 and 156 CE, covered the rest.

The Olmecs left an incredible legacy of innovations, spreading their cultural contributions through trade and establishing colonies. The Maya civilization, which emerged partway through the Olmecs' history, adopted many of their cultural elements. We owe our enjoyment of chocolate and rubber balls to these creative pioneers who introduced many historical firsts to Mesoamerica and the world.

Key Takeaways:
- Three main phases of the Olmecs
    - San Lorenzo
    - La Venta
    - Epi-Olmec and Tres Zapotes
- Firsts in Mesoamerica and the world
    - First Mesoamerican pyramid
    - First chocolate in the world
    - First rubber balls in the world
    - First to align a city according to the 260-day religious calendar
    - First glyph-writing in the Americas
    - First Mesoamerican city
    - First Mesoamerican aqueduct
- Unique cultural contribution: colossal heads

Chapter 2: The Maya

Who were the Maya, and why were they such brilliant influencers of Mesoamerican culture? And is it Maya, Mayas, or Mayan? To answer the second question, most of today's scholars use Maya (never Mayas, even when plural). Mayan refers to the language family of the Maya, which includes twenty-eight languages that are used today, such as K'iche,' Mam, and Tostsil (Tzotzil).

The Maya independent city-states spread through the Yucatán Peninsula, southern Mexico, Guatemala, Belize, Honduras, and El Salvador. Although the Maya never unified into a political empire, they shared the Mayan language family and a common culture. The Maya are among the world's oldest continuous civilizations, from their inception as a complex society around 950 BCE to the present, albeit with periods of decline and near collapse.

The early Maya settled in agricultural villages, growing corn in Mesoamerica's Formative or Preclassic period (1900 BCE–250 CE). Around 1500 BCE, the southern Guatemala Maya developed the "nixtamalization" process: soaking corn in water with a chunk of heated limestone. Nixtamalization enabled the ground corn meal to form a dough for making tortillas. More importantly, it increased the availability of niacin, an essential B vitamin. Corn nixtamalization spread throughout Mesoamerica, where it is still used today.

Around 950 BCE, the Maya built their first known ceremonial center, Ceibal, in Guatemala's Petén region at the Yucatán Peninsula's base. The Maya built Ceibal about 750 years after the Olmec built El Manatí and slightly earlier than La Venta. Ceibal was continuously inhabited for two thousand years, with a maximum population of ten thousand. In its earliest phase, the Maya built an artificial plateau at least twenty feet high and about one-half mile long.[7]

In June 2020, archaeologist Takeshi Inomata, who investigated Ceibal, announced the discovery by lidar aerial survey of another Maya ceremonial center, Aguada Fénix. This center had an even more extensive artificial plateau than Ceibal, as it was nearly a mile long and at least thirty-three feet high. With an estimated establishment date between 1000 and 800 BCE, Aguada Fénix might have predated Ceibal. Aguada Fénix is in Mexico's state of Tabasco, across the border from Guatemala.

In 1930, aerial photographs revealed an ancient city hidden in the Mirador Basin jungles fifty miles north of Ceibal. Recent archaeological studies show that agricultural villages existed there as early as 1400 BCE. Around 600 BCE, the Maya began building pyramids and temples, forming the ceremonial center now known as Nakbé, which was home to the earliest ballcourt in Maya history.

The first Maya city-state was probably Kaminaljuyú, now mostly covered by the western suburbs of Guatemala City. A city-state was a large, primary city and the small towns and agricultural villages surrounding it. Sometimes, a powerful city-state would gain control over other cities, forcing them to pay tribute and provide men for the military. Each city-state had an independent government, although they might ally with other city-states in war.

Kaminaljuyú figurine of a monkey holding her baby.
Simon Burchell, CC BY-SA 4.0 <https://creativecommons.org/licenses/by-sa/4.0>, via Wikimedia Commons; https://commons.wikimedia.org/wiki/File:Museo_Miraflores_093.jpg

---

[7] T. Inomata, et al., "Artificial Plateau Construction during the Preclassic Period at the Maya Site of Ceibal, Guatemala." *PLoS One*, 2019 Aug 30;14(8):e0221943. doi: 10.1371/journal.pone.0221943. PMID: 31469887; PMCID: PMC6716660

Kaminaljuyú grew into a large city around 800 BCE. When archaeologists Edwin Shook and Alfred Kidder investigated Kaminaljuyú in the 1930s, they found over three hundred ancient buildings and thirty-five Maya towns nearby. They also discovered that the Maya had ceramic-making factories in the city, uncovering a half million broken pottery items in one location.[8]

Kaminaljuyú had the largest population in the Maya southern highlands of the Sierra Madre mountain range. Located sixty miles from the Pacific Ocean, the city served as a trade conduit for seashells and salt from the ocean. Cacao beans (used to make cocoa) and brilliantly colored feathers came from the rainforests. The Mesoamericans prized large conch shells, which they used as trumpets, and colorful smaller shells to decorate festive clothing.

Twenty-five miles east of the city was the El Chayal quarry for volcanic obsidian glass. Mesoamerica did not develop metalworking until the 7th century CE, so obsidian was a coveted product for knives and spearheads. Obsidian artifacts from El Chayal have been found in the Yucatán Peninsula and El Salvador. Kaminaljuyú also grew cotton, a sought-after product for clothing throughout Mesoamerica.

Kaminaljuyú declined around 400 BCE, the same time as the Olmec city of La Venta. For unclear reasons, other Maya urban centers in southern Mexico and the Guatemalan Highlands also collapsed in this period. Perhaps earthquakes or volcanic activity destroyed some cities, breaking down the bustling trade routes. Cities that continued, like Tres Zapotes, were no longer engaging in long-distance trade but surviving on what they could locally produce.

Although Kaminaljuyú declined significantly, it didn't end. It stumbled along for a few centuries and then bounced back, bigger and brighter than before, surviving until 1200 CE. The city displayed its recovered wealth by building clay pipes that carried drinking water through the city. A spectacular network of canals, aqueducts, and pools transformed the metropolis into a watery paradise decorated with stone carvings of fish and turtles.

The Maya Golden Age flourished in Mesoamerica's Classic period, beginning about 250 CE. About forty major Maya cities with breathtaking

---

[8] Edwin M. Shook and Alfred V. Kidder, "Mound E-III-3, K'aminaljuyu, Guatemala," *Contributions to American Anthropology and History*, Vol. 9 (53) (1952): 33-127.

temples and pyramids thrived in the jungles and highlands of southern Mexico and Central America. Maya agricultural technology included irrigation and terraced farming along hillsides. The Maya adopted the Olmec rubber balls and played games in ballcourts, as did most other Mesoamerican cultures.

Several notable Maya cities in Mexico include Cobá, which flourished in the Classic period (250-900 CE) in the Yucatán Peninsula. Located between two lakes, an impressive network of elevated limestone causeways meandered along the lakes and through the wetlands to other Maya cities, one of which was over sixty miles away. One nearby city, Ek' Balam ("Black Jaguar"), features winged men on a mesmerizing stucco façade at the entrance of the tomb of King Ukit Kan Le'k Tok', who died in 801 CE.

Ornate tomb of King Ukit Kan Le' at Ek' Balam.
Elijahmeeks at the English-language Wikipedia, CC BY-SA 3.0 <http://creativecommons.org/licenses/by-sa/3.0/>, via Wikimedia Commons; https://commons.wikimedia.org/wiki/File:Ekbalam-Jaguar-Altar-Right.png

In Maya society, kings held godlike status in the city-states they ruled. Maya rulers descended from royal dynasties, which occasionally meant a queen ruled the city-state if the royal family had no suitable male available. Royal lineage was bilateral; it could go from the bloodline of the father or the mother or both. The Maya knew their kings could get sick, injured, and die like everyone else. For them, "godlike" meant they were hybrid divine-human creatures.

The Maya did not hold the Western concept of an infinite, all-powerful, unchanging, and infallible deity. In Maya metaphysics, gods and supernatural beings were born, could die, and were vulnerable, unpredictable, and inconsistent. Their theology allowed for an imperfect, mortal king to call himself "Ajaw" (divine lord). Kings often used names associated with Maya deities, such as K'inich (sun) or Balam (jaguar).[9]

Since there was a strict divide between nobility and commoners, only the elite could wear elaborate clothing decorated with feathers and shells. In the Maya feudal system, the nobility controlled most of the farmland, and the serfs farmed it in return for part of the harvest. Kings, administrative officials, military commanders, scribes, and high priests were all part of the nobility and were literate.

In addition to clothing, Maya people demonstrated their status through cranial modifications. Newborn babies and toddlers would lie in a special cradle or have padded wooden frames tied to their heads to change the shape of their skulls. The shape of the adjusted skull depended on kinship and status. Another status symbol was drilling holes in teeth for jewelry and filing teeth into different shapes.

Examples of how the Maya shaped the skulls of their small children.
https://commons.wikimedia.org/wiki/File:Maya_cranial_deformation.gif

Commoners worked as craftsmen and merchants and served in the military. Warriors captured in battle faced one of two fates: enslavement or human sacrifice. Other people were enslaved because of crimes or debts, and orphan children were in peril of being sacrificed or enslaved. When a king or queen died, their slaves would often be sacrificed and

---

[9] Stephen Houston and David Stuart, "Of Gods, Glyphs and Kings: Divinity and Rulership among the Classic Maya," *Antiquity* 70, no. 268 (1996): 289–95. doi:10.1017/S0003598X00083289.

buried in their tombs to serve them in the afterlife.

Since the Maya civilization was never a united empire but a collection of self-ruling city-states, the kings vied for power, access to coveted resources, and control of trade routes. As with most Mesoamerican cultures, they practiced human sacrifice and needed victims, although not on the gruesome scale of the Aztecs. Maya kings fought other Maya and nearby cultures, and warfare was especially rampant from around 600 to 900 CE when several stressors hit the Maya.

Conflict arose when some cities outgrew their agricultural output. When they cleared the jungle for more farmland, that led to soil erosion in the rainy season. Other times, they didn't get enough rain; even a moderately poor harvest due to drought could have led to near starvation in the overcrowded cities. These problems would have eroded the people's trust in their rulers and increased warfare with nearby city-states in the grab for land and resources.

When the Maya went to war, they bombarded the enemy with spears, arrows, blowgun darts, and stones from slings. The Maya adopted the atlatl or spear-thrower from the Teotihuacanos of central Mexico, which used leverage for lethal power and speed. The atlatl was a shaft with a cup or notch at one end into which the spear butt fit. The warrior held the other end of the atlatl and the spear and threw it, holding the atlatl but releasing the spear. The extra leverage from the atlatl sent the spear farther and faster than if simply thrown by hand.

How the atlatl spear-thrower worked.
Sebastião da Silva Vieira, CC BY 3.0 <https://creativecommons.org/licenses/by/3.0>, via Wikimedia Commons; https://commons.wikimedia.org/wiki/File:Nativo_do_Novo_Mundo_lan%C3%A7ando_flecha_com_o_propulsor_ou_est%C3%B3lica.jpg

Hand-to-hand combat in Maya warfare was brutal. They had a three-and-a-half-foot wooden club lined with razor-sharp obsidian blades, which could knock a man out or slice his head off. The Mesoamericans started working with metals in the mid-Classic era, and the Maya added copper knives and ax heads to their deadly repertoire by 650 CE. Their objective in battle was often capturing the enemy rather than killing them so they would have victims for human sacrifice or slavery. Hence, they often used the blunt end of their battle axes to knock their opponent out instead of killing him.

Some Maya built defensive walls around their cities, although this was rare. The Maya occasionally hurled gourds filled with hornet nests at enemy lines, confusing and panicking the warriors as a cloud of angry, stinging hornets flew out. The Maya carried small, round shields made of animal skins, woven reeds, or wood. They wore quilted cotton armor with rock salt sewn into the batting to deflect or break the enemy's obsidian blades.

The Maya produced an outstanding cultural heritage of literacy. From the earliest centuries of their civilization, they erected stone stelae with simple pictograph glyph inscriptions, as the Olmecs had done. By 300 BCE, they had developed a much more sophisticated hieroglyphic written language, which they carved into altars, around doorways, and on stone pillars. They also wrote on paper made from bark and made pictorial books with accordion folds.

The Maya logo-syllabic script used pictographs (picture symbols) for nouns and action verbs and glyph symbols for prepositions and adjectives. They used phonetic symbols to represent sounds like we use consonants and vowels. A Maya scribe worked with three to five hundred characters. If writing on bark paper or animal skin, the writer wrote with feather quill pens or a brush made from animal hair. If using quills, he or she (yes, some upper-class women could write) had quills with large and small tips for the basic glyph outlines and finer details.

The Maya wrote numbers with dots and bars. Dots represented the numbers one through four: one dot was the number one, two dots were the number two, and so on. A bar represented the number five. Two bars would be ten, three bars would be fifteen, and so on. The number six would be one bar and one dot, and the number twelve would be two bars and two dots.

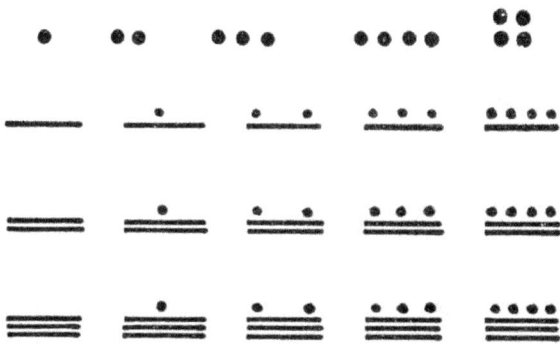

How the Maya wrote the numerals one to nineteen.
https://commons.wikimedia.org/wiki/File:Maya_Hieroglyphs_Fig_39.jpg

Like the Olmecs, the Maya used both a 260-day religious calendar (*Tzolk'in*) to keep track of special festival days and a 365-day calendar (*Haab*) for agricultural purposes. The 365-day calendar had eighteen 20-day months plus a 5-day month. Around 36 BCE, perhaps two centuries earlier, the Maya started using the Long Count calendar, which kept track of all the days since creation in cycles of fifty-two years. The Epi-Olmecs also began using the Long Count calendar by at least 32 BCE.

The Maya used a "Calendar Round" with four circles to keep track of time. Around the outermost circle was a hieroglyphic sign for each of the 18 months of their 365-day solar year cycle. Immediately inside that outer circle was a second circle with the numbers for the twenty days of the month, with zero represented by a shell. The inner two circles of the Calendar Round were for the 260-day religious calendar. The third circle from the outside perimeter had glyphs for the twenty months of the Tzolk'in religious calendar, and the fourth circle had numbers for the thirteen days of each religious month.

Each day, the Maya would place four shells or pebbles on the calendar, marking the month and day of the solar calendar and the month and day of the religious calendar. It took fifty-two years for all four circles of months and days to line up the same way again. When this happened, a new cycle began. Most Mesoamerican cultures adopted this calendar system and were using it when the Spaniards arrived in the early 1500s CE.

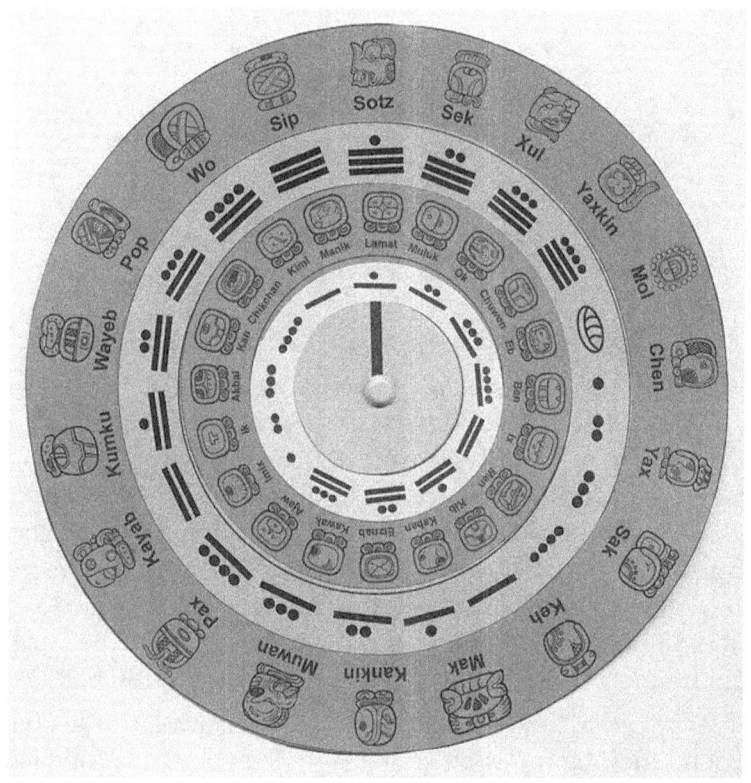

Maya Calendar Round.
Croppy Peace Sign, CC0, via Wikimedia Commons;
https://commons.wikimedia.org/wiki/File:Construction_paper_Mayan_calander.jpg

Key Takeaways:

- Who were the Maya?
    - Independent city-states sharing language family and culture
    - Settled in regions from southern Mexico to Central America
    - Early ceremonial centers and cities: Ceibal, Aguada Fénix, Nakbé
    - First city-state: Kaminaljuyú
- Maya Golden Age
    - Societal structure
        - Kings and commoners
        - Status symbols: clothing, cranial modification, tooth jewelry

- Warfare
    - City-states vying for power and access to land and goods
    - Weaponry, armor, and defense tactics
- Cultural heritage
    - Logo-syllabic script
    - Numbers
    - Calendar Round

Mexico's highest Maya pyramid (243 feet tall) at Toniná in Chiapas State.
Dge, CC BY-SA 4.0 <https://creativecommons.org/licenses/by-sa/4.0>, via Wikimedia Commons; https://commons.wikimedia.org/wiki/File:Tonin%C3%A1_(150).jpg

Chapter 3: The Zapotecs

They called themselves the Cloud People, the Ben 'Zaa, because they believed their ancestors descended from the clouds and that their spirits would ascend into the clouds when they died. The Cloud People dominated the Oaxaca Valley of southern Mexico for almost two millennia before the Aztecs arrived and called them "Zapotec." That name either meant "cloud merchants" or "people of the sapote tree," a type of persimmon common in the area. The Zapotec language family, still spoken with over fifty languages, is part of the Otomanguean language group, which includes the Mixtec languages.

The earliest significant Zapotec settlement was San José Mogote, about seven miles northwest of today's Oaxaca City.[10] The Zapotecs were the first to establish villages and make pottery in the Oaxaca Valley, and their Gray Ware ceramics later became a sought-after trade item. The Zapotecs developed into a complex civilization by 1300 BCE, erecting ceremonial buildings in San José Mogote surrounded by defensive stake fences. Their cultural advancements were several centuries ahead of the Maya and about five hundred years behind the Olmecs.

They began using irrigation ditches to enhance farming in the semi-arid region and constructing adobe buildings by 850 BCE. They developed trade networks, importing obsidian from the Guadalupe Victoria region in

---

[10] Susan T. Evans, *Ancient Mexico and Central America: Archaeology and Culture History* (London: Thames and Hudson, 2004), 122.

Puebla and El Chayal in Guatemala.[11] By 600 BCE, San José Mogote evolved into a socially stratified chiefdom of about one thousand people living on fifty acres, controlling forty nearby villages and towns. The stone-block ceremonial structures at San José Mogote were oriented eight degrees west of north. This alignment was the same as the Olmec city of La Venta 250 miles away, a trade destination for the iron oxide mirrors the Zapotecs produced.[12] By 500 BCE, San José Mogote had declined as Monte Albán sprang to power about twelve miles south.

Zapotec core area.
Photo modified: zoomed in. https://commons.wikimedia.org/wiki/File:Zapotecos.png

The Oaxaca Valley is a rough Y-shape, with three regional divisions of the Zapotec civilization, each with its own subset of the Zapotec language family. The Valley Zapotecs were located in the central Oaxaca Valley and held the most potent political power. The Sierra Zapotecs lived in the mountains north of the Oaxaca Valley, not far from Olmec territory. The Southern Zapotecs lived near the Pacific coast. For most of their history, the Southern (Pacific Coast) Zapotecs were independent of Monte Albán. Differences in pottery styles and decorative motifs showcase the cultural divide between the three sub-groups. Imports from other Mesoamerican regions differed, indicating the three areas had separate trade destinations.[13]

The Valley Zapotecs led the way in cultural innovations in the Oaxaca Valley. A carving with two glyphs found in San José Mogote dated to 650 BCE. Around 500 BCE, the Zapotecs of the Monte Albán area developed

---

[11] Arthur A. Joyce, "Interregional Interaction and Social Development on the Oaxaca Coast," *Ancient Mesoamerica* 4, no. 1 (1993): 69. http://www.jstor.org/stable/26307326.

[12] Evans, *Ancient Mexico and Central America*, 122-3.

[13] Joyce, "Interregional Interaction," 71.

Mesoamerica's first complex hieroglyphics in the logo-syllabic system. This language development was close to when the Oaxaca Valley people segued from scattered chiefdoms into a more centralized and powerful government.

The Zapotec hieroglyphics were similar to the later Mayan hieroglyphics in that they both had pictorial symbols for nouns and action verbs and phonetic symbols for sounds. Yet, unlike the Mayan script, which read in blocks from right to left, the Zapotec script read from the top to the bottom of the page like ancient Chinese characters. The Zapotec stopped using their writing system by 900 CE, embracing the Mixtec and later the Aztec script. The old Zapotec script wasn't deciphered until 2022. In 2018, archaeologists discovered a fifty-foot frieze dating to between 650 to 850 CE in the Monte Albán archaeological site with the largest number of Zapotec glyphs ever found. Three years later, scholars completed a rough translation of the script, which included calendar notations.[14]

Like the Maya, the Zapotecs used bars and dots to represent numbers. They also used the 260-day sacred calendar, the 365-day solar calendar, and cycles of 52 years. They kept historical records of their calendars with notations for lunar and solar eclipses and might have calculated the timing of eclipses. The Saros eclipse cycle of 6,585 days, when the sun, moon, and earth return to almost a straight line, nearly coincided with 25 cycles of their 260-day sacred calendar.

Monte Albán served as the Zapotecs' first capital beginning around 500 BCE when the Zapotecs built it on top of a mountain about 1,300 feet above the Oaxaca Valley. Monte Albán means "white mountain" in Spanish; the Zapotecs called it Daní Baan, or "sacred mountain." Its elevated position provides a view of the surrounding valley, making it a superb defensive location. Although there is no evidence of a previous settlement on the summit, it might have served as an earlier ceremonial location.

The food supply for the mountaintop city came from the valley below. The valley was well suited for agriculture since there was no frost, a high water table that made irrigation easy, and flat land with little erosion. The Zapotecs leveled off their mountaintop and built a paved ceremonial

---

[14] Jane Recker, "Researchers Decipher the Glyphs on a 1,300-Year-Old Frieze in Mexico," *Smithsonian Magazine*, March 8, 2022. https://www.smithsonianmag.com/smart-news/researchers-decipher-the-glyphs-on-a-1300-year-old-frieze-in-mexico-180979691/

center. Temples and palaces sat on raised platforms next to a sunken ballcourt, and thirty-foot-high walls surrounded the city. The temples were two-roomed structures with porticos in the front.

Monte Albán's mountaintop ceremonial center.
https://commons.wikimedia.org/wiki/File:Ruins_field.jpg

More than three hundred stone slabs that date back to the city's beginnings depict rubbery, contorted men that early archaeologists naively called *danzantes* or "dancers." Closer inspection revealed closed eyes and gaping or grimacing mouths. Furthermore, Mesoamerican men usually covered their genitals, but these men were completely naked, and some were castrated. The men weren't playfully dancing—they were dead. Perhaps they were captured warriors who became sacrificial victims. A similar stone slab at San José Mogote shows a disemboweled man.

Intriguingly, some of the men have beards. Ancient Mesoamericans rarely wore beards, except the Olmecs. Did the carvings represent Olmec men? The Olmec civilization collapsed around 400 BCE, about a century after the Zapotecs built Monte Albán. The two cultures traded goods, and the Zapotecs adopted aspects of Olmec culture, such as ballcourts. But the violence portrayed in the carvings suggests a war between the Olmecs and Zapotecs.

The Zapotecs of Monte Albán enjoyed a friendship with the gigantic metropolis of Teotihuacan in the Basin of Mexico, about three hundred miles northeast of the Oaxaca Valley. Zapotecs began migrating to

Teotihuacan by 200 BCE during the massive city's earliest days. Perhaps the Zapotecs were among the multiethnic city's founders. They had an Oaxacan barrio on the southwestern side of the city with fifteen Zapotec apartment compounds where they manned workshops producing Oaxacan Gray Ware pottery. The Zapotecs also lived alongside the Teotihuacanos in the Chingú, Acoculco, and El Tesoro colonies in Hidalgo, which were only 60 miles northwest of Teotihuacan but 330 miles from Monte Albán. The Zapotec population living with the Teotihuacanos in Hidalgo were probably from the Zapotec enclave in Teotihuacan.[15]

Archaeologists divide the city's history into four phases. Monte Albán I began in 500 BCE when the urban center was first built, perhaps by people who had moved out of San José Mogote. It controlled one thousand villages and small towns scattered throughout the Oaxaca Valley. Monte Albán II ran from 100 BCE to 200 CE when the Zapotecs began colonizing to the north and south of the Oaxaca Valley in what became the Sierra Zapotec and Southern Zapotec territories. Monte Albán III was the 200 to 500 CE era when the city's population grew to twenty-five thousand and was at its zenith of power. In Monte Albán IV (500–1000 CE), the city's influence declined as other cities in the Oaxaca Valley rose in power. By 1000 CE, Monte Albán was a ghost town.

Huitzo (San Pablo Huitzo) lay in the northernmost tip of the Oaxaca Valley at the border between the Mixtec and Zapotec territories divided by the Garcés River. Small farming villages dotted the area by 1000 BCE, and around 400 CE, the Zapotecs established a town with a fortress on top of a hill. Images of the Feathered Serpent deity, Quetzalcoatl in the Aztec Nahuatl language, decorated the citadel.

As with other agricultural centers in the Oaxaca Valley, the farmers of Huitzo used a pot-irrigation system. They buried unglazed, narrow-necked clay pots up to their rims in the fields next to where squash, tomatoes, chilis, or other plants grew. They kept the pots filled with water, and when the surrounding soil dried out, it created a suction force from soil moisture tension. The water in the pots seeped through the clay, disbursing water to the plant roots. For large grain fields, like maize, the Oaxaca Valley farmers used canal irrigation.

---

[15] Haley Holt Mehta, "Colonial Encounters, Creolization, and the Classic Period Zapotec Diaspora: Questions of Identity from El Tesoro, Hidalgo, Mexico" (PhD diss., Tulane University, 2019), 47-53.

The Zapotecs practiced an "infield-outfield" agricultural system, relying on the annual flooding of rivers in the rainy season. The "infield" was the land closest to the river; the flooding brought fresh soil, renewing nutrients. In the "outfield" areas unreached by flooding, they used slash-and-burn cultivation, burning off the corn stubble or other remaining plants after the harvest. The fire left a nutrient-rich layer of ash that fertilized the soil. Since mountains on three sides surrounded the town of Huitzo, the farmers built terraces up the mountainsides to enlarge their farming areas.

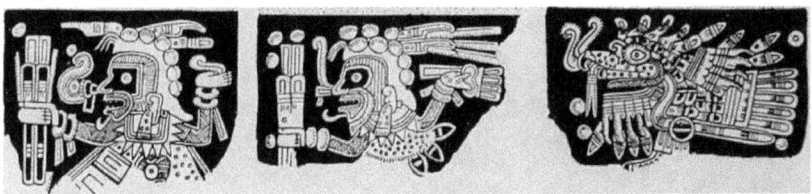

Zapotec deities on a Mitla tomb fresco, with the Feathered Serpent on the right.
Internet Archive Book Images, No restrictions, via Wikimedia Commons;
https://commons.wikimedia.org/wiki/File:Ancient_civilizations_of_Mexico_and_Central_America_(1917)_(18009178109).jpg

The mountain city of Mitla was a sacred Zapotec burial site with intricate stone mosaics not found elsewhere in Mexico. Early Zapotecs lived in the area from 900 BCE, and it grew into a city and powerful religious center by 450 CE, eventually replacing Monte Albán as the Zapotec capital. Instead of pyramids, Mitla features eight enormous, flat-roofed rectangular buildings called the Group of the Columns, which are renowned for their geometric relief carvings.

The Postclassic Zapotecs displayed engineering genius with complex designs on Mitla's Group of the Columns and massive blocks over the doorways. Trachyte volcanic-rock columns supported the roofs, and polished stone, cut and fitted together without mortar, formed "stepped-fret" geometric designs on the walls. The buildings, originally painted red, served as a palace and temple complex where regular human sacrifice occurred. The high priest's throne, covered with a jaguar skin, sat in one of the temples.

"Stepped-fret" geometric designs on a Mitla building.
Roman Israel, CC BY-SA 4.0 <https://creativecommons.org/licenses/by-sa/4.0>, via Wikimedia Commons; https://commons.wikimedia.org/wiki/File:Puerta_mitla_fachada.jpg

The Zapotecs lived immediately south of their neighbors and sister culture, the Mixtecs. The two groups frequently battled each other, especially as the Mixtecs grew stronger in the Postclassic age and began encroaching on Zapotec territory. But then, a new adversary arrived. The Mexica-Aztecs in the Basin of Mexico allied with two other Aztec tribes in 1428 CE. Within months, the new Aztec Empire invaded the Oaxaca Valley, conquering Mixtec strongholds and engaging the Zapotecs in several wars in which the Aztecs were victorious.

But then, the Aztecs faced their own ultimate nemesis when Spanish ships sailed toward the Mexican coast in the early 16th century. After the Spaniards brutally defeated the Aztecs, the Zapotecs decided upon a strategy of non-resistance. Nevertheless, the Zapotecs suffered huge losses from diseases the Spaniards introduced to the Americas, against which the indigenous people had no acquired immunity. The Spaniards forced them to convert to Catholicism, building churches on top of former Zapotec temples. But the Zapotec people survived, with about 400,000 still living in the Oaxaca Valley, many speaking their ancient languages.

Key Takeaways:
- Earliest settlement: San José Mogote
  - Complex civilization by 1300 BCE
  - Chiefdom of over forty towns
  - Oriented eight degrees west of north like La Venta
- Three divisions: Sierra Zapotecs, Valley Zapotecs, Southern Zapotecs
- Literacy and calendar
  - Logo-syllabic script
  - Recorded and possibly calculated eclipses with the sacred calendar
- Key Zapotec sites
  - Monte Albán: capital
  - Huitzo: an agricultural center
  - Mitla: the second capital
- Conquest by Mixtecs, Aztecs, and Spaniards

Chapter 4: The Mixtecs

With stunning turquoise and gold jewelry, exquisitely painted ceramics, and deerskin fold-out books chronicling their history, the Mixtecs left an indelible imprint on ancient Mexico. Like their sister culture, the Zapotecs, the Mixtecs called themselves the "cloud people" or "Nusabi," which the Aztecs translated into "Mixtecatl." Their culture stretched back to 1500 BCE, yet they didn't rise to power until the Zapotecs peaked in the 8th century of the Common Era.

The Mixtecs had three geographic groups with distinct cultures speaking over thirty related languages. The first group to emerge was the Mixteca Alta, who established terraced farming around 1500 BCE. This densely populated culture lived at chilly elevations of up to 8,200 feet in the Sierra Madre del Sur range in today's states of Oaxaca and Guerrero. Some Mixtecs spread to the valley regions of northwest Oaxaca and the southwestern part of Puebla, known as the Mixteca Baja. Eventually, the Mixteca de la Costa settled along the Pacific coast of Guerrero and Oaxaca.

Before the early Mixtecs had cities, they were trading with the Olmecs, as archaeologists found Mixtec ceramics in the Olmec heartland and Olmec artifacts in Mixtec territory.[16] One of the Mixtec's earliest cities was Etlatongo in the northeastern Oaxaca state, which they built in approximately 500 BCE over an abandoned ceremonial center. The

---

[16] Kent V. Flannery and Joyce Marcus, "Las Sociedades Jerárquicas Oaxaqueñas y el Intercambio con los Olmecas," *Arqueología Mexicana*, 87, (2007): 73.

Olmecs might have constructed the earlier center almost a thousand years previously, as Olmec-type figurines were in the area.

Archaeologists recently uncovered an exciting find in Etlatongo: two ballcourts dating to approximately 1374 BCE. These ballcourts were there *before* the Olmecs constructed San Lorenzo but after they built El Manatí, both of which had rubber balls but no known ballcourt. Scholars are now wondering who made these ballcourts. Was it the Olmecs or another mysterious advanced civilization?[17]

Around 500 BCE, the Mixtecs built Monte Negro across the high mountains northeast of the Oaxaca Valley. With a population of 2,900, the city's temples and other buildings had limestone foundations and columns, adobe walls, and thatched roofs. Like the Maya, the Etlatongo and Monte Negro elite used cranial modification to mold their children's skulls into rounded coneheads. The Mixteca Alta built Tilantongo, or Temple of Heaven, in the northwestern Oaxaca Valley around 300 BCE, which eventually became the Mixtec capital under King Jaguar Claw.

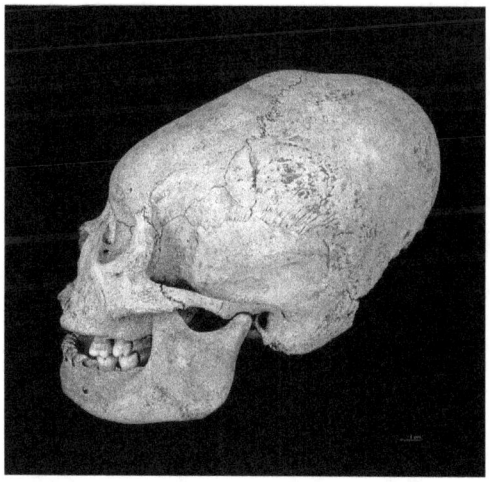

Modified Mixtec skull found in Monte Negro.
Muséum de Toulouse, CC BY-SA 4.0 <https://creativecommons.org/licenses/by-sa/4.0>, via Wikimedia Commons;
https://commons.wikimedia.org/wiki/File:D%C3%A9formation_P%C3%A9ruvienne_MHNT_Noir.jpg

Around 250 CE, in the early Classic era, the Mixtec began spreading into the valleys of Oaxaca and Puebla, entering into their Ñuiñe cultural

---

[17] J. P. Blomster and Chávez Salazar, "Origins of the Mesoamerican Ballgame: Earliest Ballcourt from the Highlands Found at Etlatongo, Oaxaca, Mexico," *Science Advances* 6, no. 11 (March 13, 2020). doi: 10.1126/sciadv.aay6964. PMID: 32201726; PMCID: PMC7069692.

phase. Their new proximity to the Zapotecs meant a strong crossover between cultures. For instance, the glyphs in the Ñuiñe writing system were similar to what the Zapotecs were using in Monte Albán, but the Mixtecs had a distinct way of combining symbols. The Mixtecs' trade with the metropolis of Teotihuacan led to cultural exchange, especially in ceramics and artwork.

As time passed, the Mixtecs formed kingdoms that were established on political and marriage alliances among royal dynasties. As the Zapotec culture declined around 800 CE, the Mixtecs reached the apex of their civilization. The Mixtec were as likely to fight each other as they were to fight other civilizations. However, they began expanding farther south, aggressively assimilating Zapotec territory and gaining control of the Oaxaca Valley. The Mixtecs didn't eliminate the Zapotecs, but they forced them to pay tribute and sometimes lived with them in the same cities. The Mixtecs took possession of the mostly abandoned Zapotec capital of Monte Albán around 1350, considering it a sacred place where they buried their own royalty.

The Mixtecs occasionally had female rulers; perhaps the most notable was Queen Six Monkey of Huachino. As archaeologist Daniel Hipolito noted in his article "Art of War," Queen Six Monkey sallied forth into battle wearing her quechquémitl (a poncho-like garment) with a snake design.[18] After she conquered the enemy, the Codex Seldon shows her wearing a garment decorated with seven black, red, and white arrows, a sign of elevated sociopolitical status. Hipolito also remarked that the Mixtec Codex Zouche-Nuttall recorded female warriors defeating mythological creatures.[19]

For centuries before the Spaniards arrived, ancient Mixtecs created pictorial books recording their genealogies, history, mythology, and religious beliefs. Like the Maya, they used deerskin or paper from tree bark, forming fold-out books called codices (singular: codex). The Aztecs also produced codices, but they burned most of theirs during a revisionist history phase and lost many more when the Spaniards burned their cities.

---

[18] Daniel Santos Hipolito and Jose Antonio Casanova Meneses, "Armas Mixtecas Acercan al Público al Arte de la Guerra entre los Mixtecos durante el Posclásico," *Instituto Nacional de Antropología e Historia* 36 (February 2018). https://inah.academia.edu/DanielSantosHipolito

[19] Daniel Santos Hipolito and Jose Antonio Casanova Meneses, "Armas Mixtecas Acercan al Público al Arte de la Guerra entre los Mixtecos durante el Posclásico," *Instituto Nacional de Antropología e Historia* 36 (February 2018). https://inah.academia.edu/DanielSantosHipolito

Most of the surviving pre-Hispanic codices are Mixtec.

The Codex Bodley was twenty-two feet long when completely unfolded. It recorded some royal lineages, which were integral since the Mixtecs believed their nobility descended from the gods. The Mixtecs considered their kings and queens as intermediaries between the gods and people; thus, preserving the bloodlines by only marrying other royals with divine ancestors was imperative. The Codex Bodley also included creation stories and exploits of their legendary monarchs.

Although the royal families of the various city-states intermarried, the Mixtec city-states often vied for power with each other. Their codices recorded pivotal wars between the major players: Jaltepec, Suchixtlan, Tilantongo, Tlaxiaco, Tututepec, and Yanhuitlan. The artist/scribes who painted the codices employed bright colors and minute details, using red lines to divide the page and guide the reader through a maze of unfolding stories. The style of writing varied among the Mixtec regions.

A revered Mixtec tale found in the Codex Bodley and the Codex Zouche-Nuttall recorded the feats of the renowned 11th-century king Eight Deer Jaguar Claw of Tilantongo. "Eight Deer" was the day and month of his birth, a typical naming practice among the Mixtec. He ruled from 1084 to 1115 CE and became the only king to unite the Mixtecs of the mountains, valley, and coast, creating a formidable empire.

His city of Tilantongo was one of the oldest Mixtec cities, but it was still a leading city in the Postclassic era (900–1521 CE). In his first year as king, Jaguar Claw made a pilgrimage to the mountain city of Chalcatongo to pay homage to the goddess of death and elicit her backing in his empire-building schemes. His first target was the mighty city of Tututepec, about two hundred miles south of Tilantongo near the Pacific Ocean.

At this time, Oaxaca's Pacific coast region had a small population but fertile land for growing cotton. Valuable resources from the ocean included fish, salt, and seashells (with which the elite loved to decorate their clothing). The area also had rainforests where the Theobroma cacao trees grew. The Mesoamericans made chocolate from cacao beans; they even used them as currency. The brilliant red and green quetzal birds also lived in the rainforest, and the elite Mesoamericans coveted their feathers for elaborate headdresses and clothing.

Jaguar Claw and his brother, Twelve Earthquake, successfully conquered Tututepec. In a grand ritual with the high priests and nobles, Jaguar Claw moved the goddess of death to a temple on Bird Hill in

Tututepec. Controlling the coast brought unimaginable wealth to Jaguar Claw and his empire, as they traded priceless resources throughout Mexico. Beginning in 1095, Jaguar Claw and Twelve Earthquake resumed their expansion campaign. In two years, they conquered twenty-five cities, mainly of the Chatinos, a branch of the Zapotecs. At the end of their campaign, the goddess (or priestess) Lady Nine Grass proclaimed Jaguar Claw the *yaha yahui* or high priest of the Mixtec, giving him the power to shapeshift into an animal or the wind.

The Toltecs, who ruled from Tollan three hundred miles north, colonized Cholula in Puebla. Cholula's Toltec king was Jaguar Four, Face-of-the-Night, and in 1097, he sent four ambassadors to Jaguar Claw, proposing an alliance. The Mixtecs and Toltecs played a ritual ball game to celebrate their union, which Jaguar Claw's team won. After Jaguar Claw helped to expand Toltec territory in Puebla, he traveled to Cholula for a grand ceremony. The Toltecs rewarded him with a turquoise nose ring, symbolizing his position as the Mixtec emperor.

Face-of-the-Night and Jaguar Claw from the Codex Zouche-Nuttall.
https://commons.wikimedia.org/wiki/File:Oaxaca_ocho_venado.png

Jaguar Claw's half-sister, Jade Fan, was his lover until she was married to his mortal enemy, King Bloody Jaguar. When Jaguar Claw was forty, he married Jade Fan's daughter, Thirteen Serpent. In 1101 CE, he conquered his hated father-in-law's city and killed him and most of Bloody Jaguar's brothers, sparing only the youngest, Four Wind. That was a poor decision, as Four Wind led a coalition army against Jaguar Claw fourteen years later. Four Wind took him prisoner and sacrificed him.

Mixtec artisans were renowned for their gold metalwork and their outstanding expertise in jewelry and intricate mosaics. After they fell to the Aztecs, the Mixtecs paid an annual tribute of gold items and ten decorated human skulls to Aztec Emperor Moctezuma II. The skulls were covered with a mosaic of lignite, turquoise, and sometimes jade, with eyes of fool's gold (iron pyrite) and conch shells. Mixteca codices showed priests and kings wearing the skulls as an ornament hanging down their backs, probably representing the "smoke and mirrors" god, Tezcatlipoca.

A human skull covered with a mosaic of turquoise, jade, and lignite.
Wikipedia Loves Art participant "artifacts," CC BY 2.5
<*https://creativecommons.org/licenses/by/2.5*>, *via Wikimedia Commons;*
https://commons.wikimedia.org/wiki/File:WLA_lacma_Mosaic_Skull_Mixteca-Puebla_Style.jpg

In 1458 CE, the Aztecs conquered some Mixtec city-states while others maintained independence. In 1486, the Aztecs built a fort at Huaxyácac hill (near today's Oaxaca City), where they administered tribute payments from the Zapotecs and Mixtecs. The Mixtecs sent so much of their artistic work in tribute payments that it's difficult to discern whether Aztecs or Mixtecs made pieces found in Aztec cities.

Three decades after the Aztecs built the Huaxyácac hill fort, word spread throughout the Mixtec territory of the arrival of ships carrying men with beards. In 1521, they heard the Aztecs had fallen to the red-headed Hernán Cortés and his soldiers. Francisco de Orozco marched into the Oaxaca Valley the following month, representing the Spanish Crown. The Mixtecs submitted, mostly peacefully, having heard of the atrocities the Aztecs suffered.

Zealous Catholic priests arrived, determined to eliminate Mixtec polytheism. New diseases, such as influenza, measles, and smallpox, reduced the estimated 1.5 million Mixtecs to 150,000 by 1650. However, once the Mixtecs acquired immunity, the population bounced back. Today, about 800,000 Mixtecs live in Mexico and 500,000 in the United States, with 530,000 still speaking the Mixtec languages.

Key Takeaways:

- Nusabi (cloud people); Mixtecatl in the Aztec language
    - Kinsmen of Zapotecs in language and culture
    - Rose to power as Zapotec civilization peaked
- Development of their civilization
    - First cities around 500 BCE
    - Impacted by Zapotecs and Teotihuacanos
- Vied for control with other cultures
    - Gained supremacy over Zapotecs
    - Queen Six Monkey and other women warriors
- Mixtec culture
    - Language and writing
    - Legend of Jaguar Claw from codices
    - Exquisite turquoise and gold jewelry
- Conquest by Aztecs and Spaniards

Chapter 5: The Toltecs

The Toltecs migrated from the harsh northwestern deserts into central Mexico in the 7th century CE and built a mighty city in the Tula Valley, seventy miles north of today's Mexico City. Their capital of Tollan grew to about sixty thousand people, and its fierce warriors conquered territories until it ruled an empire of colonies stretching into southern Mexico. Although their civilization collapsed in the mid-12th century, the Toltecs left an enduring cultural legacy for the Aztecs, Maya, and other central and southern Mexican people.

Their name meant "artisan" due to their legendary skill in artistry and architecture. They were ardent followers of the feathered serpent god Quetzalcoatl; their famous king Cē Ācatl Topiltzin even took the name of this deity. Toward the end of the Toltec rule, they became notorious for frequently sacrificing people and displaying their skulls on a rack in their temple complex.

How do we know what we know about the Toltecs? Their priest Huematzin reportedly chronicled their history, including their arduous journey south to the Tula Valley, in the *Teoamoxtli* (*Things of the Divine*). The Aztecs said the book contained Toltec proverbs, laws, sacrificial rites, astrology, calendar, and philosophy. If the book really existed, it was lost. Only a few scattered glyphs in the Toltec ruins at Tollan indicate the Toltecs knew how to write, although the Aztecs said the book was pictorial. Glyphs that are central Mexican in nature appear in the Toltec section of Chichén Itzá in the Yucatán Peninsula, a city apparently built by both the Maya and Toltecs.[20]

The Aztecs either copied the book or recorded what must have been a robust oral tradition. The Mexica tribe of the Aztecs also migrated from the northwestern deserts, arriving in Tollan shortly after it collapsed. The Mexica lived in the mostly abandoned city for twenty years, absorbing its culture. They arranged marriages with the remnants of the Toltec nobility, thus claiming descent from the Toltec aristocracy. The Aztecs wrote the Codex Chimalpopoca shortly after the Spaniards arrived; it was probably a copy of an older version providing some details of Toltec history.[21]

The Acolhua-Aztecs arrived in the Valley of Mexico earlier than the Mexica-Aztecs and coexisted with the Toltecs for at least a half-century. Fernando de Alva Cortés Ixtlilxóchitl, a descendant of the Acolhua-Aztec kings, wrote *Relación Histórica de la Nación Tulteca* around 1600. He consulted the ancient codices (more might have existed at that point) and interviewed the elderly Aztec scholars, who remembered the old songs and traditions.

Diego Durán, a Dominican friar who grew up in Mexico and was fluent in Nahuatl, collected accounts from the Aztecs and read their codices. He wrote the *History of the Indies of New Spain* in the late 1500s, a record of the Aztecs and other indigenous people of central Mexico. Some scholars scoff at the Aztec accounts as mythological, and some even suggest the Toltec Empire was a baseless legend. Although parts of the Aztec accounts are fanciful, the archaeological evidence of an enormous city in the Tula Valley with distinctive architectural features is unquestionable. Moreover, the Mixtecs interacted with the Toltecs and recorded details of the empire's royalty and colonization in their codices.

---

[20] Ross Hassig, *War and Society in Ancient Mesoamerica* (Berkeley: University of California Press, 1992), 125.

[21] *History and Mythology of the Aztecs: The Codex Chimalpopoca*, trans. John Bierhorst (Tucson: The University of Arizona Press, 1992).

Pyramid B at Tula with the Atlanteans at top and colonnades at bottom.
AlejandroLinaresGarcia, CC BY-SA 3.0 <https://creativecommons.org/licenses/by-sa/3.0>, via Wikimedia Commons; https://commons.wikimedia.org/wiki/File:TulaSite104.JPG

The Toltecs were a Chichimeca tribe, the Nahuatl-speaking hunters and gatherers of northwestern Mexico's barren wastelands. According to the Aztecs, the Toltecs abandoned their nomadic lifestyle to establish the city of Huehue-Tlapallan. Eventually, two Toltec chiefs attempted to usurp power, leading to thirteen years of civil war. After losing, the two chiefs and their supporters went into exile between the mid-400s and mid-500s CE (depending on how one interprets the dates in the codices).

They traveled almost two hundred miles until they came to a land called Tlapallanconco, where they regrouped and settled for several years. Their long-lived and insightful astrologer-priest Huematzin reminded them that prosperity and power always follow persecution. He cautioned them not to stay so close to their enemies and shared his vision of a large, fertile land with few people.

The Toltecs left their older folk and young children in Tlapallanconco and set out to find that new land. They vowed to abstain from sexual relations for twenty-three years so that pregnancies and small children wouldn't impede their migration. After reaching Xalisco, which was near the ocean, they settled for eight years. Then they continued their migration, moving from one place to another until twenty-three years had elapsed. Celebrating the end of their abstinence with a big party, they resumed lovemaking and started having babies again. They continued to move on every few years but left some families behind to establish colonies.

After over a century of moving from one temporary settlement to another, they came to their final destination of Tula (or Tollan) in today's state of Hidalgo. Arriving between the mid-500s and mid-600s, the Toltecs weren't Tula's first inhabitants. The massive city of Teotihuacan, sixty miles southeast, had colonized the area for centuries. But Teotihuacan was in its final throes and was in no position to challenge the newcomers.

The high priest Huematzin was reportedly still alive, although he would have been well into his second century of life. He suggested they strike a deal with the nearby Chichimeca tribe, a different branch from the Toltecs and a potential threat. They asked the Chichimeca tribal chief to give one of his sons to be their king in exchange for leaving the Toltecs in peace. Thus, their first king was the Chichimeca prince Chalchiuhtlanetzin, who ruled for fifty-two years.

The next king was Ixtlilcuechahua, who was either Chalchiuhtlanetzin's son or the son of a Toltec chieftain, depending on the account. By this point, Teotihuacan, the one-time powerhouse of central Mexico, had collapsed, and Ixtlilcuechahua expanded Toltec dominion over the former Teotihuacan colonies. The Toltec architectural style and artifacts have been found from the Pacific to the Gulf of Mexico and into the Yucatán Peninsula, where the Toltecs migrated in several waves.

The Atlantean warriors stand sentry atop Pyramid B at Tollan.
H. Grobe, CC BY 3.0 <https://creativecommons.org/licenses/by/3.0>, via Wikimedia Commons; https://commons.wikimedia.org/wiki/File:Mexico1980-170_hg_1.jpg

Next to the old settlement of Tula Chica, the Toltecs built Tula Grande, a stunning city gleaming with jade, gold, and eye-catching sculptures and architecture. At the center of Tula Grande, also known as Tollan, stands the remarkable ruins of its ceremonial plaza, complete with a ballcourt and striking pyramids and temples. The five-tiered Pyramid B is an impressive example of the Toltecs' incredible architecture. At its top stand the nearly fifteen-foot-high Los Atlantes or Atlanteans: pillars carved in the shape of warriors holding atlatl spear-throwers that once supported the roof of a temple. In front of the pyramid are the remains of a colonnaded walkway. Rows of carvings of jaguars alternating with coyotes and eagles decorate the pyramid.

The most prominent Toltec leader was the semi-mythological Cē Ācatl Topiltzin, who ruled in the 10th century. His father was Mixcoatl, a great Toltec chieftain who was later elevated to deity status as the Aztec god of the hunt. Mixcoatl was hunting one day when he encountered a naked woman named Chimalma. For some reason, he started shooting arrows at her, but she had the power to deflect his arrows, which aroused his admiration and passion. Mixcoatl married Chimalma, who became pregnant when she swallowed a jade stone.

Mixcoatl was assassinated by his brother, and Chimalma died in childbirth, leaving the newborn Cē Ācatl Topiltzin an orphan. Chimalma's parents raised him, teaching him about the feathered serpent deity Quetzalcoatl, who was worshiped in the nearby megacity of Teotihuacan. Cē Ācatl Topiltzin was so devoted to the god that he took his name; however, he detested the human sacrifices the Teotihuacanos offered to Quetzalcoatl.

When Cē Ācatl Topiltzin Quetzalcoatl grew up, he killed his father's assassin and became the king of Tollan, encouraging the worship of Quetzalcoatl but forbidding human sacrifice. His reign was the Toltec Golden Age, a time of prosperity and peace. The city surged ahead in agricultural technology and became famous for its artistry. Migrants poured into the wealthy city, seeking a better life. For over fifty years, Cē Ācatl Topiltzin served as their king and priest. He was a wise and merciful ruler.

But then, the smoke and mirrors god, Tezcatlipoca, deceived Cē Ācatl Topiltzin with black magic by giving him a mirror. When the king looked at it, his face was distorted. Tezcatlipoca reassured him, saying, "Don't worry, just drink this potion, and you'll look normal again. Look! Here's your sister. Why don't you share the drink with her?"

The king and his sister were unaware that the drink contained hallucinogens. The following day, Topiltzin's attendants found him lying next to his sister, both naked. The king wasn't sure what had happened, but he was humiliated and horrified. He left Tollan and wandered through Mexico, cutting himself until his blood ran in a wretched attempt to purge his sin. Eventually, he reached the Gulf of Mexico.

His story has several endings. One is that Topiltzin immolated himself on a funeral pyre. As thousands of red and green quetzal birds flew out of the flames, his spirit rose into the sky to become Venus, the morning star. Another version is that he sailed on a serpent raft into the Gulf of Mexico, promising to return in a "one-reed" year, the beginning of the fifty-two-year cycle of the Mesoamerican calendar.[22] Centuries later, when Hernán Cortés arrived by ship in a one-reed year, some Aztecs thought he might be the returning Topiltzin Quetzalcoatl.

Cē Ācatl Topiltzin on his serpent raft from Fray Durán's Codex.
https://commons.wikimedia.org/wiki/File:Quetzalcoatl_on_his_raft_of_serpents.jpg

Topiltzin's abdication left a power vacuum in Tollan. Most of the city's migrant population came from cultures where human sacrifice was considered a necessary evil to maintain the balance of the cosmos. The

---

[22] *The Codex Chimalpopoca*, 26.

Toltecs had rarely practiced human sacrifice, and Topiltzin tried to eradicate it. Yet, once he was out of the picture, the new ruling class surged ahead with the gory practice. In the central ceremonial plaza stood a skull rack holding the heads of sacrificial victims whose beating hearts had been cut from their bodies. Archaeologists unearthed the skeletons of twenty-four children, ages five to fifteen, who had been decapitated in a mass sacrifice to Tlaloc, the god of rain. In another mass grave, they found forty-nine more child sacrificial victims.

The city was divided into two groups. On one side were the pro-Quetzalcoatl Toltecs, who were against human sacrifice and favored a theocracy led by a priest-king. The other side favored a military dictatorship and frequent human sacrifice to ensure success in war and protection from calamities. For centuries, internecine strife continued, flaring up and then dying down. Some Toltecs left for other places, such as the Yucatán Peninsula.

Amid the chaos, a young woman named Xóchitl caught the eye of King Tecpancaltzin when she visited the palace with her family. Her father, Papantzin, wanted to introduce the king to a beverage he'd invented called pulque, which was made from fermented agave (maguey) sap. The king enjoyed the drink and asked Papantzin to send Xóchitl with more. When Xóchitl returned with the pulque, the king detained Xóchitl and made her his concubine. Papantzin came to the palace, sputtering in rage, but Tecpancaltzin granted him lands and titles to keep him quiet. Xóchitl had a child named Meconetzin, "child of maguey," who became the crown prince since the king's wife had no sons. When Queen Maxio died, Tecpancaltzin made Xóchitl his queen.

As the palace intrigue played out, ethnoreligious conflict rocked the city over the issue of human sacrifice and whether Quetzalcoatl or the smoke and mirrors god Tezcatlipoca should be the chief deity. After decades, the schism finally reached a boiling point with a great battle in which the Tezcatlipoca faction prevailed. Xóchitl led a female battalion into combat in a desperate attempt to turn the tide of the war, but she and King Tecpancaltzin died on the battlefield.

Meconetzin, whom Ixtlilxóchitl said was also called Topiltzin, ascended the throne and apparently managed to quell the conflict. Many Quetzalcoatl followers migrated to the Yucatán, joining a thriving Toltec community there. During Meconetzin's reign, eerie omens appeared, heralding impending disaster. These omens included a deformed rabbit with what looked like deer antlers, which was followed by an epidemic that killed nine hundred people.

The last Toltec king was Huemac, who inherited a kingdom on the brink of collapse. A megadrought almost wiped out the Maya civilization of the Yucatán Peninsula and might have also impacted Tollan. The Toltecs suffered a seven-year famine, and Huemac sacrificed his children in a frantic attempt to regain the rain god Tlaloc's favor. Around 1115 CE, the Chichimeca invaded and burned the pyramids and temples.

Eventually, Huemac led most of the remaining Toltecs out of the city, and they wandered for seven years, with some of the group dispersing to the Yucatán and Puebla. Finally, they settled in the Teotihuacan settlement of Chapultepec Hill, located on the southern end of Lake Texcoco (in today's Mexico City). The Toltecs continued on in the colonies they had established in the Valley of Mexico, Puebla, and the Yucatán, but they were no longer a united empire.

Key Takeaways:
- Sources for Toltec history
    - Aztec codices, supposedly based on Teoamoxtli (Things of the Divine)
    - Fernando de Alva Cortés Ixtlilxóchitl (Relación Histórica de la Nación Tulteca)
    - Durán's History of the Indies of New Spain
- Early settlements and civilization
    - A Chichimeca tribe that migrated south
    - Arrived in Tollan (Tula) in the 6th or 7th century CE
    - King Ixtlilcuechahua expanded Toltec territory
    - Pyramid B and Los Atlantes
- Cē Ācatl Topiltzin
    - Mythical parents Mixcoatl and Chimalma
    - Reigned over a peaceful kingdom; eradicated human sacrifice
    - Abdicated throne; swore to return in a one-reed year
- Empress Xóchitl
    - From concubine to queen
    - Rode out to battle with women of Tollan

- Emperor Huemac and Toltec collapse
    - Civil war, drought, and Chichimeca attack
    - Huemac led remnants to Chapultepec

Chapter 6: The Aztecs

From their island in a swamp, the extraordinary Aztecs built an incredible empire covering eighty thousand square miles, with six million people living in around five hundred city-states. Although the Aztecs were latecomers to the Valley of Mexico, they were empowered by a strong self-identity and a vision for greatness. The Aztecs' canny ability to assimilate other cultures and adapt to rapid change catapulted them to the top. Yet their cruelty and disregard for their disgruntled provinces opened the door for their cataclysmic fall to the Spanish conquistadors.

The Aztecs were infamous for bloody and frequent human sacrifices and even cannibalism. Yet they had schools in every neighborhood, with mandatory education for all teenage boys and girls. The Mexica-Aztecs lived in a pristine city with a remarkably advanced waste-management system. They had a law code and a social welfare system for orphans, widows, the poor, the elderly, and wounded warriors. An aqueduct piped in drinking water for Tenochtitlan's population of 200,000, with dikes and dams providing ingenious floodwater control. Lacking arable land, they built floating islands to grow food for their massive population.

The Aztec origin myth began with seven tribes on the idyllic island of Aztlán. They were all Aztecs, named after their island, but the tribes were the Xochimilca, Tlahuica, Acolhua, Tlaxcalteca, Tepaneca, Chalca, and Mexica. One by one, the Nahuatl-speaking tribes left their island paradise and migrated south to the Valley of Mexico.[23] The last to go was the

---

[23]Elzey, "A Hill on a Land," 110-11.

Mexica, whose codices say they left Aztlán around 1168 CE.

When they crossed to the mainland, the hummingbird god Huitzilopochtli sang to them from the shore, telling them they were now his people. He gave them the necessary tools for their journey and made them a powerful and wealthy people, but they had to do one thing: sacrifice humans to him. So, they captured a woman and two men of the Chicomóztoc-Mimixcoa tribe and offered them to Huitzilopochtli as their first human sacrifices.

Following their new god, the Mexica-Aztecs journeyed south through the searing desert. Finally, they arrived in the densely populated Valley of Anahuac surrounding Lake Texcoco, a region with dependable rainfall and good soil. The Mexica encountered the other Aztlán tribes, but their kinsmen were unwelcoming. They had already carved out their new city-states and didn't want power struggles over resources and land.

For almost a century, the Mexica-Aztecs lived in slave-like subservience as mercenary soldiers and construction workers for their kinsmen tribes. They intermarried in an attempt to build alliances and eventually captured the island of Chapultepec from the Tepanecs. Considering the island sacred because they revered its previous Teotihuacan and Toltec inhabitants, the Mexica lived there for twenty years until the Tepanecs wrested it back. Then, they found refuge with the Colhuacan people, descendants of the Toltecs, and allied with them in a war against the Xochimilca, another Aztec tribe.

After killing thousands of the Xochimilca warriors on behalf of their overlords, the Mexica asked for the Colhuacan king's daughter, telling him they wanted to worship her as a goddess. Their idea of "worship" was bizarre and macabre: they killed and flayed her, and the Mexica high priest wore her skin. Furious, the Colhuacans came after them, determined to destroy every last man. The Mexica fled into the swamp, and while hiding out in the cattails, their god Huitzilopochtli told them to look for an eagle perched on a prickly pear cactus. They were to build their new city at that location and subjugate the surrounding tribes and cities.

The following day, they saw it. An eagle with a snake in its talons was sitting on a prickly pear cactus on an island in the marshy southwestern end of Lake Texcoco. The land belonged to the Tepanec-Aztecs, their former enemies, but they forged a new alliance: they would fight as mercenaries for the Tepanecs in exchange for the island. The Mexica built Tenochtitlan in the swamp. They connected the island with causeways to the mainland and scratched their way to the top against their rival tribes.

Diego Rivera's mural depicting the causeway leading to Tenochtitlan.
https://commons.wikimedia.org/wiki/File:El_templo_mayor_en_Tenochtitlan.png

Their first houses were reed structures, but as their wealth grew, the Mexica built homes of stone and wood. A grand ceremonial complex with a high pyramid (the Templo Mayor) topped by two temples stood in the middle of Tenochtitlan, surrounded by four districts. Around the central temple complex stood the gleaming palaces of the city's aristocrats. Tenochtitlan grew to about 200,000 people, larger than most European cities of its day. Canals intersected their island city through which the Mexica traveled by canoe.

Itzcoatl, the fourth Mexica *tlatoani*, or king, broke Tenochtitlan free of Tepanec rule and formed an empire with two other city-states. His name meant obsidian snake, and he had been quietly waiting for the right opportunity to strike. His father was the first king of Tenochtitlan, then his older half-brother, and then his brother's son, Chimalpopoca. Meanwhile, Itzcoatl formed astute alliances for his ultimate goal of throwing off the Tepanec overlordship.

By this point, the Mexica had risen in power to become the overlords of two other Aztec tribes: the Xochimilca and Tlahuica. Yet they were still technically under Tepanec overlordship. Then, the powerful Tepanec *huey tlatoani* (emperor) Tezozomoc died, and a younger son, Maxtla, staged a coup d'état and stole the throne from his half-brother, Tayatzin. Mexica King Chimalpopoca came to the aid of Tayatzin, his mother's brother, but Maxtla's men captured Chimalpopoca. They put him in a cage, where he died of strangulation, either by his own hand or by the Tepanecs.

This sudden shift in affairs thrust Itzcoatl to the Mexica throne; however, he faced an immediate crisis. Emperor Maxtla wasn't finished punishing Tenochtitlan. He blockaded the Mexica city and cut the aqueduct bringing fresh water to the citizens. He also planned to kill Nezahualcoyotl, Itzcoatl's friend and the Acolhua king of Texcoco, which was just across the lake from Teotihuacan. Nezahualcoyotl fled east to Huexotzinco, an ancient Toltec city close to Puebla, and rallied support from its king, who happened to be another friend of Itzcoatl.

Itzcoatl also asked the city of Tlacopan for help. Tlacopan was actually a Tepanec city but had fought against the usurper Maxtla and lost. They knew Maxtla would wreak his revenge, so they allied with Tenochtitlan and Texcoco for survival. King Nezahualcoyotl of Texcoco negotiated a 100,000-man, 5-city alliance against Emperor Maxtla. These city-states included Tenochtitlan, Texcoco, Tlacopan, Huexotzinco, and Tlatelolco, another Mexica city.

The Battle of Azcapotzalco from the 16ᵗʰ-century Tovar Codex.
https://commons.wikimedia.org/wiki/File:The_Battle_of_Azcapotzalco_WDL6746.png

In 1428, the coalition army conquered the hostile Tepanec cities and then laid siege to the Tepanec capital of Azcapotzalco. The army burned the capital down and sacrificed Maxtla. The military from Huexotzinco headed back home, leaving the Mexica and Acolhua cities in power, along with the Tepanecs of Tlacopan. Tenochtitlan, Texcoco, and Tlacopan formed the Triple Alliance of the three Aztec cities, agreeing to continue conquering together until they ruled all of central Mexico. Tenochtitlan and Texcoco would each get two-fifths of the tribute payments from subjugated cities, and Tlacopan would get one-fifth.[24]

And thus, the Aztec Empire was born. The original agreement was to take turns ruling the empire, but after a few years, Tenochtitlan rose to become the supreme military and political head. Texcoco developed into a brilliant cultural center, as Nezahualcoyotl gathered philosophers and scholars into his city and wrote its first law code. The king was an architect and engineer and assisted Tenochtitlan with a dike and dam system for flood control. He also designed magnificent temples and his clifftop palace in Texcoco. Tlacopan, the minor partner of the Triple Alliance, receded into the background.

Culturally, the Aztecs tended to be assimilators rather than inventors, taking some customs to grotesque extremes. They followed the Mesoamerican 365-day solar calendar, which they called xiuhpōhualli, and the 260-day ritual calendar, tōnalpōhualli. The ritual calendar was divided into twenty-day units, each with a festival dedicated to a specific deity. In the Festival of Atlcahualo, they sacrificed children from elite Aztec families to Tlaloc, the rain god. The next festival was Tlacaxipehualiztli when the priests wore the skins of sacrificial victims.

The solar and ritual calendars lined up every fifty-two years, an event that was celebrated with the New Fire Ceremony. The Aztecs enlarged their pyramids and temples, and people thoroughly cleaned their homes and tossed out old cooking pots and clothing in this time of renewal. On the night before the first day of the new fifty-two-year cycle, they would quench all the fires in the hearths and temples around the city. At the top of Mount Huizachtecatl, a high mountain that could be seen from the towns around Lake Texcoco, they sacrificed a victim and lit a bonfire. From that fire, torches were brought down the mountain to the cities, relighting the fires in each home and temple.[25]

---

[24] Richard F. Townsend, *The Aztecs* (3rd, revised ed.) (London: Thames & Hudson, 2009), 74-5.
[25] Ross Hassig, *Time, History, and Belief in Aztec and Colonial Mexico* (Austin: University of Texas Press, 2001), 7-19.

The role of religion affected all classes of Aztec society, and as a theocratic state, religion integrated with politics. The king was also a priest; his duty was to maintain balance and harmony in his city-state and the cosmos. Under the king was a hierarchy of priests, priestesses, monks, and nuns who tended the great temples in the city center and ministered in the neighborhood shrines. Most people began their days by visiting the local temples to pray to the gods.

Huitzilopochtli from the 16th-century Codex Telleriano-Remensis.
https://commons.wikimedia.org/wiki/File:Huitzilopochtli_telleriano.jpg#file

The chief Aztec deity was Huitzilopochtli, the bloodthirsty hummingbird god of war and the sun. Huitzilopochtli demanded human sacrifice in ever-increasing numbers. His worship sometimes included cannibalism of the arms and thighs of sacrificial victims. This god was specific to the Mexica-Aztecs. Other cultures did not worship Huitzilopochtli until the Aztecs gained power. As they conquered new cities and towns, they let the people worship whatever gods they wanted as long as they added Huitzilopochtli into the mix as the head of their pantheon.

Another important deity was Tezcatlipoca, the cunning smoke and mirrors god of the night. The brother and nemesis of the feathered serpent deity Quetzalcóatl, Tezcatlipoca, tricked Toltec King Cē Ācatl Topiltzin with his black magic. Worship of this god led to a horrific increase in human sacrifice. For one year before the Toxcatl festival, a handsome and strong young soldier impersonated the god. Then, the Aztecs sacrificed him as drums beat and dancers spun about and cut themselves with knives. The young man's head adorned the skull rack that could hold thousands of the grisly relics, a custom picked up from the Toltecs.

Tlaloc, the rain deity, had been worshiped by the Teotihuacanos, the Toltecs, and numerous other Mesoamerican civilizations. Like most cultures in ancient Mexico, the Aztecs portrayed him with goggle eyes and fangs. At the top of Tenochtitlan's highest pyramid, the Templo Mayor, stood two temples: one for Huitzilopochtli and one for Tlaloc, who demanded child sacrifice in exchange for rain. Elite families gave their baby boys to be drowned, with 20 percent of Tenochtitlan's children feeding the god, especially in times of drought.

Children who survived the five annual festivals involving child sacrifice would be schooled at home from ages three to thirteen. Then, teenagers of both genders attended neighborhood schools; the Mexica-Aztecs were among the first in the world to mandate education for young people. Younger children learned practical skills from their parents. Mothers taught their little girls to weave cotton and to cook. Boys went to work with their fathers to learn a trade. Their fathers also taught them how to fish and make baskets from reeds.

Around the age of fourteen, boys from the nobility attended a *calmecac* school, where they lived in dormitories and studied astronomy, reading, writing, history, religion, and war. Their training focused on positions as administrators, codex painters, medical professionals, priests, and teachers. Boys from non-elite families also lived in dorms at the *telpochcalli* schools, where they received instruction in military skills and religion. They continued training in a trade, such as craftsmanship or agriculture. Teen girls lived at home but attended day school to learn theology, dancing, and singing. Some girls received training in midwifery and other medical work.

Tenochtitlan needed a way to feed its 200,000 people living on two connected islands, so it demanded tributes of corn and other food from the provinces. For fresh vegetables, the city relied on the floating gardens, called chinampas, surrounding the city. More extensive floating gardens grew on Lake Xochimilco, which connected to Lake Texcoco's southern end. The Xochimilca sent food to Tenochtitlan by raft in tribute payments.

The lake agriculturalists built underwater supports of wooden stakes and woven reeds to form a platform on which they would pile mud dredged from the shallow lake bottom. In the mild climate, the farmers grew seven crops a year in the fertile floating gardens. When they harvested one crop, they immediately planted a new one from seedlings started on rafts. The farmers traveled by canoe around the canals that connected the floating gardens.

The Aztecs entered the Valley of Mexico as a ragtag band of nomads, but they quickly adapted to the more civilized cultures while steadily fighting their way to the top. They broke free from their overlords through canny alliances and formed a great empire. And yet, it came crashing down only a century later when the Spaniards arrived. Perhaps it would have imploded anyway, even if the Europeans hadn't invaded.

The Aztecs drained the provinces they ruled of resources without giving much in return. They drafted their warriors to fight for them and took their children as slaves and sacrificial victims. They attacked their neighbors to acquire more victims to feed their bloodthirsty gods. They also failed to realize that leadership must always look to the future, guarding its resources and stewarding its people to meet the challenges ahead.

Key Takeaways:
- Five hundred city-states and six million people
- It had a law code, waste management system, and social welfare system.
    - History overview
    - Aztlán: island of origin
    - Led by hummingbird god Huitzilopochtli
    - Subservience to other tribes for about a century
    - Formed Triple Alliance with Texcoco and Tlacopan

- Calendar System
    - 365-day solar calendar (xiuhpōhualli) and 260-day ritual calendar (tōnalpōhualli)
    - New Fire Ceremony launched a new fifty-two-year cycle
- Role of religion
    - Theocracy, where kings were also priests
    - Chief god Huitzilopochtli, the hummingbird god of war and the sun
    - Second in rank was Tlaloc, the god of rain, who demanded child sacrifice
    - Tezcatlipoca and Quetzalcoatl were other important gods.
    - Worship involved human sacrifice and sometimes cannibalism
- Mandatory education for all teen boys and girls
- Floating chinampas fed the large population

PART TWO:
Historical Periods

Chapter 7: Preclassic Mexico (1900 BCE–250 CE)

Humans lived in ancient Mexico from the days when fourteen-foot-tall Columbian mammoths roamed the Valley of Mexico. Over time, the ancient humans developed from nomadic hunters and gatherers into farmers who lived in permanent or semi-permanent villages. Some civilizations advanced faster than others, especially in fertile, well-watered areas suitable for agriculture.

The Guilá Naquitz Cave enters the base of a cliff three miles from Mitla in the Oaxaca Valley. It holds seeds dating as far back as 6000 BCE and is the oldest evidence of domesticated crops in Mexico. What were the earliest plants grown in Mexico? Squash was first, followed by maize (corn) and beans. These three plants formed the "Three Sisters" companion planting, which spread from Mexico throughout North America. The indigenous people planted beans around the corn stalks, which acted as a trellis, while the beans put nitrogen into the soil. In between the corn stalks, the people grew squash, which shaded the ground, keeping it moist.

Archaeologists divide pre-Hispanic Mesoamerican history into three major eras: Preclassic, Classic, and Postclassic. Scholars don't quite agree on exactly when each period and sub-period began and ended, but they are roughly the same. The Preclassic period extended from about 1900 BCE to 250 CE, the Classic period from 250 to 900 CE, and the Postclassic from 900 to 1521 CE.

This chapter explores the Preclassic period, also known as the Formative era, when people began making pottery, forming ceremonial centers, and building cities. The Formative period is marked by the emergence of more sophisticated agricultural methods, developing arts, and hierarchal societies. It is called "Preclassic," as the Classic period marks the beginning of megacities, such as Teotihuacan, with elaborate art and architecture.

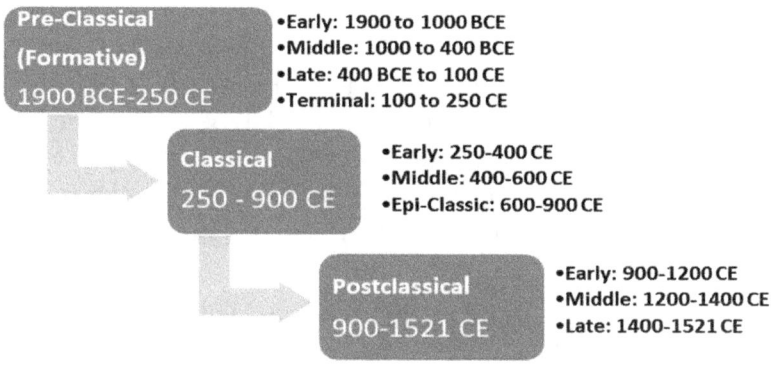

A handy guide to the Mesoamerican eras.

The Preclassic era has four sub-divisions: the Early Formative (1900-1000 BCE), the Middle Formative (1000-400 BCE), the Late Formative (400 BCE-100 CE), and the Terminal Formative (100-250 CE). The ancient people of Mexico learned to form clay into pots and fire them in pits or open bonfires at the beginning of the Early Formative era. Scholars analyze the distinctive types of pottery to identify the historical periods and the civilizations that made them.

Puerto Marqués and La Zanja, south of Acapulco Bay in Guerrero, could be the sites of Mexico's earliest known pottery. Archaeologist Charles Brush called it "Pox Pottery" because small pits marked the inside of the vessels, possibly caused by wiping the interior as the clay dried. Using radiocarbon analysis, he dated the Puerto Marqués ceramics to 2400 BCE. However, a recent excavation dated similar pottery from Puerto Marqués to between 1820 and 1400 BCE.

Nine hundred miles down the Pacific coast from Puerto Marqués is Paso de la Amada in the state of Chiapas in the Mazatán region near Guatemala's border. Beginning in about 1900 BCE, the Mokaya people settled in this area, producing round, neckless *tecomate* pottery jars. The

Mokaya entered their Locona phase around 1650, with more variety in their ceramics, including figurines.

The Locona phase also marked the beginning of chiefdoms and large-scale architecture and when Paso de la Amada became a regional ceremonial center. The Mokaya built Mexico's first known ballcourt with a sunken compacted earthen floor around 1650 BCE. It had rows of earthen benches on each side of the narrow alley-like playing field, which was about 250 feet long, 22 feet wide, and open at each end.[26]

Two hundred miles south of Paso de la Amada is Chiapa de Corzo on the Pacific coast. The Zoque people settled here around 1400 BCE, developing sophisticated hieroglyphic writing at about the same time as the Maya. From 1200 to 600 BCE, Chiapa de Corzo was one of Mexico's largest urban centers, with a strong connection to the Olmecs, judging by pyramids and pottery styles. The local Zoque people might have been vital trade partners or colonized by the Olmecs, whose core area was 160 miles north.

Based on La Venta's alignment, archaeologists believe the Olmecs used the 260-day ritual calendar by 800 BCE. The first written date, corresponding to December 36 BCE in our calendar, was in Chiapa de Corzo on "Stela Two," apparently inscribed by the Epi-Olmecs. The Olmec Cascajal Block found close to San Lorenzo demonstrated that the Olmecs were using simple glyphs by the late 10th century BCE. The Epi-Olmecs developed the more sophisticated Isthmian script. A potsherd found in Chiapa de Corzo dating to approximately 300 BCE is the earliest example of the Epi-Olmec text and parallels the emergence of the Mayan logo-syllabic script.

Chiapa de Corzo has the oldest pyramid tomb, dating between 700 to 500 BCE. A priest or king around fifty years old lay in state in a stone chamber inside the pyramid with a one-year-old baby on his chest. Another male, around eighteen years old, was unceremoniously tossed into the tomb. He was likely a servant sacrificed to serve his master in the afterlife. On a landing outside the tomb lay a middle-aged woman, probably his wife. The man and woman wore jade collars, their bodies were draped with pearl, jade, and amber ornaments, and their mouths were filled with precious jewels. Olmec-type ceramics were in the tomb, but the stone walls and wooden roof were a Zoque innovation.

---

[26] Blomster and Salazar, "Origins of the Mesoamerican Ballgame."

While the Mokaya, Olmecs, and Zoque flourished in the south, Tlatilco emerged as an early chiefdom center in the Valley of Mexico around 1250 BCE, about thirty miles north of today's Mexico City. Its sister city of Tlapacoya, southeast of Mexico City, was founded earlier, around 1500 BCE. The Tlatilco were prosperous trade partners with the Olmecs and were known for their peculiar terracotta figurines.

The Tlatilco "pretty-lady" figurines had thin waists, broad hips, balloon-like thighs, and usually no feet or hands. The ceramic statuettes were about six inches tall and sometimes wore ballerina-type skirts. They had slanted eyes. Some wore hoop earrings, and most had a braided coif or a cap. Some were pregnant or holding a child, suggesting a fertility cult, and a few figurines had two or three faces. The Tlatilco culture faded away by 800 BCE for unclear reasons.

Tlatilco figurines dating from 1300 to 1000 BCE.
Madman2001, CC BY-SA 4.0 <https://creativecommons.org/licenses/by-sa/4.0>, via Wikimedia Commons; https://commons.wikimedia.org/wiki/File:Tlatilco_culture_figurines.jpg

About 250 miles south of the Valley of Mexico, the Zapotec civilization emerged about the same time as the Tlatilco civilization. The Zapotecs erected their first ceremonial buildings in San José Mogote about 1300 BCE, which eventually grew into a city-state of one thousand people ruling over forty nearby villages and towns. The Zapotecs used glyphs by 650 BCE and developed sophisticated hieroglyphics by 500 BCE.

Although the Maya culture emerged by at least 1900 BCE, their first-known ceremonial centers were Ceibal in Guatemala and Aguada Félix in

Tabasco, Mexico, which were built between 1000 and 800 BCE. Their first city-state was Kaminaljuyú on the western side of today's Guatemala City, which grew into a large city around 800 BCE. The Maya carved glyphs in stone stelae by 900 BCE and developed their logo-syllabic script, which had picture symbols and phonetic symbols, by 300 BCE.

The Valley of Mexico's first city-state with a social hierarchy was Cuicuilco on Lake Texcoco's southern shore. It was settled by 1200 BCE. The city of twenty thousand people ruled over several large towns by 800 BCE. Cuicuilco had an aqueduct piping fresh water into the city, as well as irrigation canals and pyramids. The city's population began declining around 100 BCE, probably due to volcanic activity and competition with the rapidly growing metropolis of Teotihuacan, which was forty-five miles northeast. In the late 3rd century, a massive eruption of the Xitle volcano buried Cuicuilco under a thick layer of lava and ash.

The Mixtec culture emerged to the north of the Zapotecs around 1500 BCE. The highland Mixtec "Alta" built their earliest cities of several thousand residents at Etlatongo and Monte Negro in 500 BCE. Around 300 BCE, they constructed Tilantongo, which later became the Mixtec capital. The Mixtec did not develop into a more sophisticated civilization with writing until the Classic era when they moved into the Oaxaca Valley, close to the Zapotecs.

Teotihuacan formed into an urban center in the northeastern Valley of Mexico by at least 200 BCE. Its population eventually grew to a massive size, yet it collapsed around 650 CE, leaving few clues as to who built this metropolis and how it was governed. The Aztecs thought the gods or maybe giants created the city. The Totonac people of Puebla and Veracruz claimed to have been the original builders who then migrated south after the city fell. The Totonacs did have cultural and trade links to Teotihuacan, so they might have been among its early inhabitants.

Archaeologists Tatsuya Murakami and George Cowgill suggested that several civilizations cooperated in establishing the city in what they called *synoikism*. The goal might have been forming a united front against Cuicuilco, the Valley of Mexico's powerhouse at the time.[27] The valley's scattered, decentralized settlements might have united with the Totonacs, the remnants of the Olmecs, and the Zapotecs.

---

[27] Matthew Robb, ed, *Teotihuacan: City of Water, City of Fire* (Berkeley: University of California Press, 2017), 21.

Cowgill, who spent most of his career excavating and studying Teotihuacan, said that by 1 BCE, the city's population reached forty thousand. The Teotihuacanos had not yet built their three great pyramids or their apartment compounds, but it might have been the largest city in Mexico at the beginning of the Common Era, certainly the largest in the Valley of Mexico. By 100 CE, Teotihuacan had grown to eighty thousand people, and the initial construction of the Pyramid of the Moon was completed, although it would be enlarged several times.

A flurry of energetic building projects transformed Teotihuacan in the Terminal Formative era, perhaps under the leadership of a potent dictator or a series of ambitious monarchs. From 150 to 200 CE, the Teotihuacanos built the ornate Feathered Serpent Temple and the thirty-eight-acre Ciudadela courtyard surrounding it. A row of feathered serpent heads projected out from each layer of the pyramid, alternating with a fanged, goggle-eyed creature, perhaps a crocodile deity or the rain god. Construction of the Pyramid of the Sun, which towered over the city as Mexico's highest pyramid at the time, might have begun around 200 CE.

Vista of Teotihuacan from the Moon Pyramid, with small temples in the foreground, the Avenue of the Dead, and the Sun Pyramid in the background.
Johannes Kruse, CC BY 2.0 <https://creativecommons.org/licenses/by/2.0>, via Wikimedia Commons; https://commons.wikimedia.org/wiki/File:Teotihuacan_(cropped).jpg

Most of the Valley of Mexico's population migrated into Teotihuacan after 100 CE. By 200 CE, Teotihuacan's population reached its apex of 125,000 to 200,000 people. The surrounding region, extending out twenty miles from the city, tripled in population. Migrants also came from outside the Valley of Mexico, as the Maya, Mixtecs, and more Zapotecs were drawn to the flourishing economic hub. The various ethnic groups formed barrios, which housed workshops producing their specialties in ceramics, obsidian crafts, jewelry, clothing, and more.[28]

The many distinct civilizations of the Preclassic age shared several religious ideologies. All primary Mesoamerican cultures of the Formative era worshiped the jaguar, the largest feline in the Americas. As a creature of the night, the jaguar was the god of the underworld but also the god of water and fertility. The Teotihuacanos kept captive jaguars, which they sacrificed at the dedication of their pyramids. The Olmecs had carvings of "were-jaguars," creatures with cleft heads and grimacing mouths, often with partial human child characteristics. The Maya believed the jaguar god protected people.

Most civilizations in central and southern Mexico worshiped the sun, moon, and a feathered serpent, which the Yucatán Maya called Kukulkan. The Preclassic Cuicuilco, Maya, and Teotihuacan cultures worshiped an old man deity, who is often depicted sitting cross-legged and balancing a brazier on his head. He is thought to have been a fire god. The storm, rain, and war god, which the Aztecs later called Tlaloc, pervaded Preclassic cultures. He was the benevolent god of rain and fertility yet the destructive god of hurricanes, lightning, and hail. He also demanded child sacrifices. Most ancient Mesoamericans practiced animal and human sacrifice.

Although religious beliefs in the various cultures of ancient Mexico evolved as the centuries passed, they shared a common worldview and many similar deities. The core Mesoamerican belief system of the Preclassic era continued through the Classic and Postclassic periods until the Spaniards arrived. Many ancient Mexican cities were aligned with where the sun rose on specific days in the shared ritual calendar. Pyramids and other temples in the middle of cities were worship centers where priests and kings offered sacrifices. The ancient people believed that deities influenced every aspect of their lives. Thus, keeping the gods happy was a driving force in their everyday traditions and monthly festivals.

---

[28] Cowgill, "State and Society,"129.

Key Takeaways:
- Early civilizations
    - Guilá Naquitz Cave: first domesticated crops in Mexico, circa 6000 BCE
    - Puerto Marqués and La Zanja: first ceramics in Mexico, circa 2400 BCE, maybe later
    - Paso de la Amada: Mesoamerica's first ballcourt, circa 1650 BCE
    - Chiapa de Corzo: first written date (36 BCE), first pyramid tomb (700 BCE)
    - Tlatilco culture: Valley of Mexico's first chiefdom; known for ceramic figurines
- Zapotecs
    - Established San José Mogote in 1300 BCE, grew to one thousand people and ruled forty towns
    - Using glyphs by 650 BCE and logo-syllabic hieroglyphics by 500 BCE
- Maya
    - First ceremonial center in Mexico, Aguada Félix in Tabasco, 1000-800 BCE
    - First used simple glyphs by 900 BCE, sophisticated hieroglyphics by 300 BCE
- Cuicuilco, the first city-state with a social hierarchy in the Valley of Mexico: 1200 BCE
    - Population of twenty thousand by 800 BCE with aqueduct, irrigation, and pyramids
    - Covered by lava flow from Xitle volcano in 3rd century CE
- Teotihuacan, established between 400 and 200 BCE
    - Multiethnic city probably from the outset
    - Population of forty thousand by 1 BCE, probably the largest city in Mexico at the time
    - 100 CE: population up to eighty thousand; Moon Pyramid built

- o Feathered Serpent Pyramid was built between 150 and 200 BCE
- o 200 BCE: population at least 125,000; Sun Pyramid possibly begun
- Common religious ideologies of Preclassic Mexico
  - o Jaguar deity
  - o Sun, moon, feathered serpent, old man/fire god, rain god

Chapter 8: Mexico in the Classic Period (250–900 CE)

The Teotihuacan megacity dominated the Valley of Mexico in the Classic era, while Monte Albán ruled the Oaxaca Valley and Cholula the Puebla region. Several Maya city-states in the Yucatán and Mexico's southern border were at their zenith, such as Palenque in Chiapas, Edzna in Campeche, and the nearby "Snake Kingdom" of Calakmul. The collapse of Teotihuacan, Cholula, and Monte Albán in the Epi-Classic (Late Classic) age left a power vacuum for other cities to fill, including Xochicalco in Morelos, Cacaxtla in Tlaxcala, and El Tajín in Veracruz.

At the onset of the Classic period, Teotihuacan grew into the largest city in the Western Hemisphere, with the sixth-highest population in the world. Through thriving coast-to-coast trade and sometimes conquest, it was the powerhouse of Mesoamerica from 300 to 600 CE. Majestic pyramids, palaces, and temples with spectacular murals and sculptures lined its magnificent Avenue of the Dead, which ran on a north-south axis through the megacity's core. Teotihuacan was a commercial hub, with over six hundred workshops producing highly prized ceramics, jewelry, weaponry, and clothing.

Teotihuacan launched an incredible construction project in the early Classic era, erecting about 2,300 one-story apartment complexes for its massive population. Each walled compound housed up to one hundred people, with a large courtyard at its entrance featuring a small temple for worship and brilliant murals on the walls. The people living within each compound were usually kinsmen or shared the same ethnicity. The compounds were like a series of enclosed villages within the metropolis, providing a safe place for children to play and a sense of belonging.

Teotihuacan had distinct neighborhoods for its various ethnicities. For instance, the Maya lived in the city's center, just west of the Avenue of the Dead. People from the Gulf Coast lived in the Teopancazco barrio southwest of the urban center, and a large Zapotec population lived on the far western side. Each of these barrios had workshops producing regional specialties. The Zapotecs created Gray Ware pottery, while the Gulf Coast population sewed cotton clothing decorated with bright feathers and shells for the elite. Other barrios produced knives and spearheads from razor-sharp volcanic obsidian glass, exquisite jewelry, and various goods, which were traded throughout central and southern Mexico, Guatemala, Belize, and Honduras.

The old man god sits in a shrine with brilliantly painted murals.
Gary Todd, CC0, via Wikimedia Commons;
https://commons.wikimedia.org/wiki/File:Teotihuacan_Mural_%26_Stone_Brazier.jpg

Between 250 and 400 CE, the Teotihuacanos enlarged the Moon Pyramid at the northern end of the Avenue of the Dead three times. Anthropologists Ruben Cabrera and Saburo Sugiyama discovered a vault in the pyramid's core in 2004, where they found fifty sacrificed animals, including eagles, jaguars, pumas, wolves, and rattlesnakes. They also uncovered the skeletons of twelve humans, ten of whom were decapitated. They had been sacrificed at the dedication of the third layer of the pyramid. More renovations of the Moon Pyramid continued about every fifty years until 400 CE, when it reached its final height of 140 feet.

The Pyramid of the Moon stood at the northern end of the Avenue of the Dead, the city's central boulevard, and the Feathered Serpent Pyramid stood at the southern end. The 216-foot Pyramid of the Sun, built around 250 CE, towered in the middle and was visible from all points of the metropolis. The Aztecs misnamed it; the pyramid probably wasn't dedicated to the sun but more likely to the goggled-eyed rain god to whom children were sacrificed. Archaeologists found the remains of sacrificed babies and young children with images of the rain god in a vault under the pyramid. They found more child skeletons on all four corners of each of the pyramid's layers.[29]

Teotihuacan had friendly trade and diplomatic relations with the Zapotec city of Monte Albán, which was three hundred miles southeast. Hundreds of Zapotecs lived in the Oaxacan barrio in Teotihuacan, and some Teotihuacanos lived in Monte Albán. Stone stelae inscriptions in Monte Albán document diplomatic visits from Teotihuacan. Both cities reached their apex and then collapsed at about the same time.

By 500 CE, Teotihuacan's population declined, and the city ultimately collapsed around 650. The causes of the city's downfall are unclear; however, centuries earlier, civil unrest of unknown origins rocked the megacity. Around 350 CE, some craftsmen abruptly abandoned their workshops, leaving their tools behind. At about the same time, the Teopancazco barrio experienced massive human sacrifice or violent struggle. One-third of the buried men had been decapitated.

Anthropologist Linda Manzanilla spent eight years unearthing the Teopancazco neighborhood and believes tension and competition between the city's multiple ethnicities led to unrest. She thinks the workshop craftsmen clashed with the wealthy businessmen who were the liaison between the government and the workers. Between 550 and 650 CE, another riot erupted. Unruly crowds burned and vandalized the palaces, temples, and administrative centers along the Avenue of the Dead but left the living quarters unharmed.[30]

---

[29] Nawa Sugiyama, et al., "Inside the Sun Pyramid at Teotihuacan, Mexico: 2008–2011 Excavations and Preliminary Results," *Latin American Antiquity* 24, no. 4 (2013): 403–16. http://www.jstor.org/stable/23645621.

[30] Linda R. Manzanilla, "Cooperation and Tensions in Multi-ethnic Corporate Societies Using Teotihuacan, Central Mexico, as a Case Study," *Proceedings of the National Academy of Sciences*, 112, no. 30 (March 2015): 9214-15. https://doi.org/10.1073/pnas.1419881112

Another probable cause for tensions in the city was drought caused by global cooling, which led to food shortages. Global climate change entered an acute phase in the Northern Hemisphere in 536 CE, and temperatures remained abnormally low for about a century. Cooler temperatures meant less rain, and the springs that Teotihuacan depended on for irrigation dried up, creating an agricultural crisis and food shortages. In this period, a high rate of stillborn babies and child mortality in Teotihuacan underscored the near-famine conditions. Analysis of burials in one barrio showed almost one-third were stillborn or newborn babies. Less than 40 percent of children reached their teens, and most adults died by their mid-forties.

The world's largest pyramid by volume, bigger than anything in Egypt, lies in Cholula, thirty miles southeast of the rumbling 3.37-mile-high El Popocatépetl volcano. Today, the Tlachihualtepetl pyramid is overgrown with vegetation, looking like a small mountain with a colonial-era multi-domed church perched on top. But at one time, it was a massive adobe brick structure measuring 984 feet wide by 1,033 feet long at its base.

Just outside today's city of Puebla, Cholula was established around 200 BCE or earlier, about the same time as Teotihuacan, seventy miles north. Cholula's original inhabitants were probably related to the Zapotecs and Mixtecs, but the remnant of the Olmecs had a considerable influence. Regular summer rain and runoff from the snowy mountains meant the inhabitants of Cholula enjoyed flourishing agriculture. Its alluvial soil had a high clay content, and the region became renowned for its pottery.

Cholula was a trade hub between the Valley of Mexico and the Yucatán Peninsula. At the end of the Formative era, the city surged in population while the surrounding areas emptied, similar to how Teotihuacan simultaneously attracted a migrant population. This period was when Cholula's people began the first phase of their great pyramid and continued enlarging it in four major stages over the next six centuries.

Cholula entered the Classic era as the dominant force in the Puebla region, building the second pyramid structure, called the Pyramid of the Painted Skulls, between 250 and 300 CE. It had the talud-tablero architecture associated with Teotihuacan, indicating a strong influence from the megacity. This talud-tablero pyramid layer featured murals of red and yellow skulls with insect-like bodies. The first and second pyramids, which were adjacent to each other, were eventually encompassed by much larger pyramid layers that covered them both.

Connected to the pyramid is a mausoleum with the remains of a man and woman buried with lavish grave offerings and the jawbone of a Xoloitzcuintle (Mexican hairless) dog. Twenty-four tunnels, totaling five miles, wind through and under the pyramid, where archaeologists found a sculpture of the goggle-eyed, fanged rain god called Tlaloc by the Aztecs. Child sacrifices indicate the rain god was worshiped at the pyramid, although it is also associated with the feathered serpent deity. In the Postclassic era, some Toltecs migrated here when Tula fell and buried their royalty in the pyramid.

The Maya of Mexico reached the pinnacle of their civilization in the early Classic period and then experienced a hiatus followed by another wave of growth in population and culture. By the late 200s, the Maya extensively used their logo-syllabic script and included dates on their inscriptions on stone pillars and slabs (stelae). Vaulted or arched architectural features are a hallmark of Maya architecture in the Classic era.

The Palenque palace tower with a corbel arch at the lower left.
Bernard DUPONT, CC BY-SA 2.0 <https://creativecommons.org/licenses/by-sa/2.0>, via Wikimedia Commons; https://commons.wikimedia.org/wiki/File:The_Observation_Tower_-_Palenque_Maya_Site,_Feb_2020.jpg

A stunning example of this architectural feature is the A-shaped corbel arches in Lakamha (called Palenque by the Spanish) in Chiapas. Under K'inich Janaab' Pakal, who became king at age twelve in 615 CE and ruled until his death at eighty, the city attained staggering prosperity. Despite ongoing warfare with Calakmul, he initiated an ambitious building project of temples and palaces. One palace had a four-storied tower and corbel arches, which were novel architectural features in Mexico.

Palenque's great rival Calakmul was about two hundred miles northeast in the rainforests at the base of the Yucatán Peninsula. The kings of both city-states claimed divine ancestry and called on the nobility of the towns and cities over which they ruled to provide warriors for their military clashes. Calakmul's "Snake Kingdom" dynasty persisted for one thousand years, and some of the richest royal Maya tombs are in this resplendent city.

In 562 CE, Calakmul conquered the mighty Maya city of Tikal in Guatemala, which the Teotihuacanos had previously invaded in 378 CE and ruled for several generations. Calakmul ascended as the Maya superpower under the leadership of King Sky Witness (r. 561–572). In 599, his son, Scroll Serpent, attacked Palenque, sparking an ongoing war between the Calakmul Snake Kingdom and the Palenque Bone dynasty, with Palenque losing most of the battles. Within a century, Calakmul's mini-empire stretched southeast to Belize, with unimaginable wealth flowing into the city from its lucrative trade routes. Breathtaking murals covered the Chiik Nahb pyramid depicting trade exchanges and consumption of luxury goods.

A mural from Calakmul's Chiik Nahb pyramid.
Elelicht, CC BY-SA 3.0 <https://creativecommons.org/licenses/by-sa/3.0>, via Wikimedia Commons; https://commons.wikimedia.org/wiki/File:Calakmul_Fresken.JPG

The megacity of Teotihuacan in the Valley of Mexico collapsed in the Epi-Classic era (600–900 CE), leaving a power vacuum that enabled other cities to rise in power. Cacaxtla in Tlaxcala and Xochicalco in Morelos apparently allied in this period to snatch the trade routes that Teotihuacan once controlled. The Olmeca-Xicalanca founded both cities. They were a people with strong Maya influence who originally lived in the Olmec Gulf Coast areas and eventually migrated north.

Brilliantly painted in scarlet, blue, green, and gold, well-preserved murals from Cacaxtla depict battle scenes between Maya and highland people. The Gulf Coast Maya are shown with flat foreheads from cranial modification and feathered headdresses, and they fight against warriors wearing jaguar skins and long nose plugs. One figure representing the Eagle Lord has a blue face mostly covered by a bird mask and rides on a feathered-serpent raft as a quetzal bird flies upward.[31]

The Eagle Lord rides the Feathered Serpent in this Cacaxtla mural.
HJPD, CC BY-SA 3.0 <https://creativecommons.org/licenses/by-sa/3.0>, via Wikimedia Commons; https://commons.wikimedia.org/wiki/File:Cacaxtla2.jpg

New regions rose to dominance in the Epi-Classic or Terminal Classic age as the Zapotecs, Teotihuacanos, and some Maya cities faded. This period's vibrant art and architecture reflect an eclectic cultural blending on a grand scale. New population centers emerged, trade routes changed, and

---

[31] Donald McVicker, "The 'Mayanized' Mexicans." *American Antiquity* 50, no. 1 (1985): 82-101. https://doi.org/10.2307/280635.

innovation surged in this time of migration and shifting political landscapes.

Key Takeaways:
- Teotihuacan: the powerhouse of Mesoamerica in the Classic period
  - The largest city in the Americas, sixth largest in the world
  - 2,300 one-story apartment compounds and over 600 workshops
  - The moon pyramid enlarged multiple times with human and animal sacrifices
  - 216-foot Pyramid of Sun dedicated to the rain god
  - Global cooling, reduced rainfall, food shortages, rioting, and collapse by 650 CE
- Cholula: largest pyramid in the world; close connection to Teotihuacan
- Classic age Maya: pinnacle in Classic era with a hiatus in the middle
  - Palenque in Chiapas: corbel arches, high tower, rival of Calakmul
  - Calakmul in Campeche: conquered Tikal in Guatemala and extended to Belize
- Xochicalco and Cacaxtla
  - Rose to power as Teotihuacan collapsed
  - Settled by the Olmeca-Xicalanca

Chapter 9: Postclassic Mexico (900–1521 CE)

Chaos, warfare, and the decline of many prominent city-states marred Postclassic Mexico. And yet, it was a time of dynamic technological advances in engineering, architecture, and weaponry. The population grew exponentially, and in many ways, life was better than ever before in ancient Mexico. But at the end of the era, Mexico was fractured, suffering from oppressive overlords and unbridled human sacrifice. The city-states were unprepared to unite against the Spanish invaders.

As the Maya of the Yucatán Peninsula rose in power during the Postclassic era, they had to find reliable fresh water for their growing cities. The peninsula's northern half has no above-ground rivers, and the lakes' saline content makes the water unsuitable for drinking or watering crops. The Yucatán does have an underground freshwater aquifer accessible by numerous sinkholes throughout the region. These sinkholes are called cenotes. Some of these cenotes form a large half-circle as part of the Chicxulub crater created by a prehistoric asteroid; the rest of the crater is in the Gulf of Mexico.

Chichén Itza exploded into power in the Postclassic era, ruling most of the Yucatán Peninsula. It had four cenotes with plentiful fresh water. One of the sinkholes, the Sacred Cenote, had steep limestone walls, making it difficult to climb out if a person was thrown in. This cenote was a sacrificial place where men and boys were fed to the rain god Chaac. In recent years, divers have found a treasure trove of gold and jade objects at the bottom of the sinkhole, as well as human skeletons.

Several migrations of Toltecs from Tula between 900 and 1200 CE are reflected in Chichén Itza's architecture, particularly its El Castillo Pyramid. It was dedicated to Kukulkan, the Maya name for the feathered serpent deity whom the Aztecs called Quetzalcoatl. Archaeologists recently found a fifth cenote under this pyramid. It was full of sacrificial items, including human remains. The pyramid is aligned with the sun, so the setting sun on the spring and fall equinoxes casts a shadow leading to a sculpture of the Feathered Serpent's head at the bottom. It seems as if the serpent's shadow is slithering down the pyramid on those two evenings of the year.

Temple of Kukulkan (El Castillo) in Chichén Itza.
Carlos Delgado, CC BY-SA 3.0 <https://creativecommons.org/licenses/by-sa/3.0>, via Wikimedia Commons; https://commons.wikimedia.org/wiki/File:Chich%C3%A9n_Itz%C3%A1_-_17.jpg

Maya cities in the Yucatán that didn't have the advantage of cenotes connected to the underground aquifer had to find other ways to control and contain water. They carved enormous underground cisterns out of the underlying rock, which they covered with stucco to keep the water from seeping into the porous limestone. They arranged their cities so that water flowed from the higher areas into the cistern during the six months of heavy rain, keeping an adequate water supply for the six dry months.

But once they had a steady water supply, the Yucatán Maya had a new problem. They liked painting their buildings with red paint, but the rain gradually washed the paint off the buildings and into the cisterns. The mercury in the paint caused grave health issues, brain damage, and sometimes death. The Yucatán Maya made an engineering breakthrough when they discovered that the negatively charged mineral zeolite was like a magnet for the positively charged mercury. It could draw mercury out of the body and out of the water. So, they built a water filtration system with zeolite gravel and quartz sand wrapped in reed mats through which the water flowed as it entered the cistern. They wouldn't have known about negatively charged and positively charged minerals, but they discovered that zeolite purified the water and used it as a filter.

The island city of Xaltocan at the center of Lake Xaltocan in the Valley of Mexico, which was established around 800 CE, grew in power as the capital of the Otomi people from 1200 to 1395 CE. Some of the Toltec survivors of Tollan fled to Xaltocan. Together with the Otomi people, they launched an energetic engineering project to dredge the lakebed sediment to expand their island and construct the floating chinampas gardens. Centuries later, the Mexica-Aztecs adopted this system for their island capital of Tenochtitlan. The Codex Chimalpopoca tells of a violent conflict between Xaltocan and the Tepanec-Aztec city-state of Cuautitlán, which the people of Xaltocan eventually lost in 1395. They were forced to abandon their island.

By this point, metallurgy was developing in Mexico, which wasn't the game-changer for Mesoamerican weaponry that one would expect. Metalwork with copper, silver, and gold reached western Mexico from South America between 600 and 800 CE, especially among the Mixtecs. As the Mixtec and other metalsmiths developed innovative technologies and alloys, they achieved greater strength in metals. By 900 CE, they were blending copper and tin to make bronze.

Their initial interest was the beauty and colors of various metals in artwork, but metal's practical use in everyday implements like axes, fishhooks, and needles soon became apparent. Curiously, most of the ancient Mexican civilizations delayed applying metals to weaponry. The two exceptions were the Maya, who used copper knives and axe heads by the late Classic era, and the Purépecha (called Tarascans by the Spaniards) of the Pacific coast, who used copper shields and spearheads.

Most Mesoamericans used stone, jade, flint, and obsidian for knives, arrowheads, and spearheads up until the Spanish arrived. Obsidian glass was sharper than razor blades and highly lethal, although easily breakable. Non-metal blades were deadly enough when pitted against the quilted armor and wicker shields of Mexico's indigenous people, but they were not deadly against the Spaniards' steel armor.

One well-known Postclassic weapon used by the Aztecs was the macuahuitl, a three-foot wooden club with rows of embedded obsidian blades. The Aztecs have the most notoriety for using this weapon, but the Mixtecs, Maya, and Toltecs brandished the macuahuitl before the Aztecs even arrived in the Valley of Mexico. The sharp obsidian blades could slice off a man's head or disembowel a horse, a strategy the Aztecs later learned when fighting against Spanish cavalry.

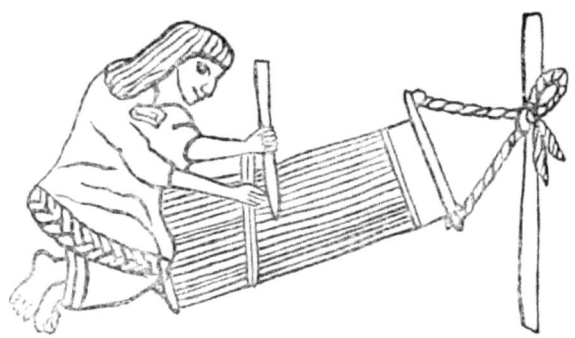

Drawing of a woman weaver from the Codex Mendoza (circa 1541).
https://commons.wikimedia.org/wiki/File:A_glimpse_of_Guatemala_-_A_Woman_Weaving.png

Cotton cloth may not seem remarkable, but it played a vital role in ancient Mexico's economy. Cotton spinning and weaving technology took off in Mexico's Postclassic age. Ancient indigenous people began spinning cotton into thread with simple spindle whorls: disks with a hole in the middle. A weaver inserted a thin wooden rod called a spindle into the hole and then pulled out a bit of fiber from a wad of cotton and attached it to the spindle. Holding on to the fiber, the weaver spun the whorl, which twisted the cotton into thread that was then woven into cloth on a backstrap loom.

The region of Morelos in the Puebla area was well known for growing and spinning cotton. Several important new devices made cotton spinning easier and faster, which increased production levels. Excavations at Xochicalco in Morelos show the Epi-Classic weavers used a more sophisticated spindle whorl beginning around 1100 CE. Spindle whorls found in Tula are similar to what the indigenous Huastec people on the Gulf Coast still use today. Around 1200 CE, weavers began using a small ceramic bowl into which they inserted the spindle, increasing the spinning speed.[32]

In the Classic era, weavers only needed to produce enough cloth for their families and to sell for profit. However, once the Aztecs rose to power and their empire swallowed up Morelos, they demanded a large quantity of woven cotton cloth as tribute payments. The women spent most of their days weaving to meet the quota, so advanced technology that could speed up the time required to spin cotton eased their burden.

The ruins of the ancient city of El Tajín lay hidden away in the Veracruz rainforest for five centuries before being rediscovered in 1785. While other urban centers collapsed, El Tajín reached its peak at the beginning of the Postclassic period, covering four square miles with a population of about twenty thousand. The city introduced novel architecture to Mesoamerica, such as key-pattern decorations, columns with intricate reliefs, windows in homes, and a poured cement roof almost one meter thick.

El Tajín's dramatic Pyramid of the Niches introduced two architectural features: window-like niches lining each of its seven stories capped by triangular flying cornice overhangs. Originally painted crimson with black niches, the 365 niches represented the days of the solar year. The Totonac people, who claim to have built Teotihuacan, currently live in the El Tajín region and might have constructed the city. However, some scholars believe the Huastec people might have been the city's founders. While most Mesoamerican cities had ballcourts, El Tajín had seventeen, more than any other.

El Tajín's Pyramid of the Niches.
Irvin ulises, CC BY-SA 3.0 <https://creativecommons.org/licenses/by-sa/3.0>, via Wikimedia Commons https://commons.wikimedia.org/wiki/File:Piramide_de_los_nichos.jpg

---

[32] Michael E. Smith and Kenneth G. Hirth, "The Development of Prehispanic Cotton-Spinning Technology in Western Morelos, Mexico," *Journal of Field Archaeology* 15 (1988): 349-355.

The hallmarks of Postclassic Mexico were population migrations and growth, most notably in the Valley of Mexico, where the population grew to an estimated one million. Waves of Chichimeca people migrated from the northwestern deserts, while the populations of collapsed cities moved to the still thriving urban centers, forming blended ethnicities. The Maya abandoned many of their majestic cities in southern Mexico and Central America, partly due to a drought between 800 and 900 CE, which shifted their power to the Yucatán.

The Postclassic era also appears to have been a time of political experimentation. In the Classic era, the Yucatán Maya had a theocratic priest-king governance, but in the Postclassic period, models of dual rulership or rule by a council (oligarchy) might have emerged. Some archaeologists believe that Chichén Itza had a "multepal" council of elite rulers; however, this theory lacks firm evidence. The Postclassic Maya stopped recording details about their kings on stone stelae, which hints that they didn't have single monarchs but decentralized leadership.

As anthropologists Jeremy Sabloff and William Rathje noted, without a dominant dynastic elite, energy was no longer expended on building towering monuments to glorify their kings. They believe that growth in trade and productivity led to collective wealth and a higher standard of living for everyone in a thriving economy. Their field research of Cozumel, an island off the Yucatán coast, provided valuable information about the Postclassic Maya. It was an important trading center and reached its peak growth in the Postclassic era through the influence of merchants rising in power and influence.[33]

The Postclassic Yucatán Maya carried out long-distance trading via large canoes along the Gulf Coast. Christopher Columbus reported spotting such a canoe off the Honduras coast in 1502. The Maya produced a high quantity of salt in the Yucatán, which was in high demand as far away as the Aztec capital of Tenochtitlan in the Valley of Mexico. Cacao beans for making chocolate were another sought-after trade item.

This flourishing trade reached from the Valley of Mexico down the Gulf and Pacific coasts into Central America, creating an interconnectedness between the various cultures. Sabloff and Rathje believe this was the highest volume and most extraordinary trade

---

[33] Jeremy A. Sabloff, "It Depends on How We Look at Things: New Perspectives on the Postclassic Period in the Northern Maya Lowlands," *Proceedings of the American Philosophical Society* 151, no. 1 (2007): 11–20. http://www.jstor.org/stable/4599041.

diversification ever seen in Mesoamerica up to that point. The massive trade of luxury goods throughout Mexico was no longer for the elite. The working class now had access to chocolate, obsidian, and fine goods, which led to a more egalitarian society.[34]

Key Takeaways:
- Technological advances
    - Aligning the pyramid with the sun to cast a "slithering snake" shadow
    - Underground cisterns with water purification systems
    - Development of metallurgy
    - Deadly macuahuitl war club
    - Sophisticated cotton spinning spindle and bowl
    - El Tajín novel architecture: niches, flying cornices, poured cement roof
- Possible new administrative models: dual rulership and oligarchic councils
- Trade improved life from the Classic to Postclassic periods

---

[34] Sabloff, "New Perspectives on the Postclassic," 20-26.

PART THREE:
The Fight for Ancient Mexico

Chapter 10: Preparing for Battle

For thousands of years, the Mesoamericans fought for power, access to valuable resources, and victims to sacrifice to their gods. As the 16th century dawned, they would have to fight for their survival when the Spaniards set foot in Mexico, determined to reap the gold and other wealth the land offered. Several momentous battles before and after the Spanish arrived changed the course of Mexico's history. Certain rituals revolved around warfare, and ambassadors, messengers, and spies contributed to how the battles played out. The "Flower Wars," military societies like the Eagle and Jaguar warriors, and the weaponry of ancient Mexico all played a part in warfare as well.

Since all able-bodied Aztec men were warriors, a special ritual celebrated a newborn boy's future role. Four days after his birth, the midwife bathed the baby in the early morning sun, and the infant received his name. The midwife placed a small arrow in the baby's right hand and a miniature shield in his left. An elite warrior would then take the arrow, shield, and the child's umbilical cord and bury it next to a deceased warrior who was a fearless fighter.

Aztec warriors could achieve high social status regardless of their family background if they were courageous, skillful, and adept at capturing the enemy alive. All Aztec boys attended mandatory schools where military training was paramount. Superior warriors won admission to one of the warrior societies and could work their way up in rank and honor. The critical factor was successfully capturing enemy soldiers for slaves and human sacrifices.

When a soldier captured his first enemy fighter, he became part of the Tlamani warrior society. He received a shield, a macuahuitl war club, two capes, and a red loincloth to mark his new status. Like all elite warriors, he tied his hair into a bun with a red ribbon. Capturing two enemy fighters took him to the next level, the Cuextecatl society. Then, he wore a bodysuit and a conical hat and carried a round shield, all in scarlet with black parallel lines.

Three captured warriors elevated him to the Papalotl or Butterfly warrior status. Although it seems strange to equate butterflies with war, the Aztec goddess of war was Ītzpāpālōtl, or "Obsidian Butterfly." Aztec warriors believed if they died in battle, they would be reincarnated as butterflies or hummingbirds. The Butterfly warriors wore a white tunic, carried a yellow shield, and wore the honorable butterfly banner on their backs.

A jaguar knight in the Codex Magliabechiano brandishes a macuahuitl club.
https://commons.wikimedia.org/wiki/File:Jaguar_warrior.jpg

When a warrior captured four or more enemy soldiers, he became a Cuauhocelotl fighter, joining the ranks of the Jaguar and Eagle knights. The Jaguar knights stood out with a bodysuit of jaguar or ocelot skin and a "helmet" of the big cat's head. Feathered bodysuits clothed the eagle warriors, and they wore a helmet shaped like an eagle's head. The elite Jaguar and Eagle knights carried atlatl spear-throwers, macuahuitl war clubs, spears, and colorful shields. A commoner automatically joined the nobility and was awarded land if he achieved this rank. He also received the right to drink the alcoholic pulque, wear flashy jewelry, and keep concubines in addition to his wife.

The top-notch military ranks were the Otomi and the Shorn Ones. These warriors were the special forces with the highest training. The Otomi warriors, named after the fierce Otomi ethnic group, wore bright emerald green bodysuits and "claw" banners on their backs topped with brilliant green feathers. The Shorn Ones were the highest level. They shaved their heads except for a long braid hanging down the left side of their heads. They wore a yellow bodysuit and a white shell necklace. The Shorn Ones carried a yellow and green shield and a red and white striped back banner topped with green feathers.

The Aztecs had a system of relay runners posted about every two and a half miles on the empire's main roads. The runners ran full speed to the next runner, delivering messages between cities or military stations. The Aztecs also used two types of spies. The *quimichtin* spies wore the clothing and spoke the language of a targeted region. Before invading, these Aztec spies scoped out the kinds of defense, military strength, and other factors of a region. The *naualoztomeca* spies were tradesmen who traveled abroad, selling and buying goods while picking up valuable information in the marketplaces.[35]

When the Aztecs targeted a city, they sent ambassadors offering peaceful admission into the Aztec Empire. The city had twenty days to decide. If they were still wavering, a second entourage of delegates visited, warning of the horrors the city faced if they resisted. If the city didn't surrender after another twenty days, the Aztecs ruthlessly pounced, demolishing the city and taking the people as slaves and sacrificial victims.[36]

The Maya, Teotihuacanos, Toltecs, and Aztecs used the atlatl spear-thrower or dart-thrower. The Aztecs only permitted royalty and the elite warriors to use this tool that flung *tlacochtli* (small spears or darts) at a high velocity toward the enemy. The *Tequihua,* the Aztec archers,

---

[35] Hassig, *War and Society,* 51-52, 165.
[36] Hassig, *War and Society,* 160.

fashioned five-foot-long simple bows called *tlahhuītōlli* out of one piece of wood from Buddleja butterfly bushes, with animal sinew for string. Another weapon was the *tēmātlatl* sling, which was woven from maguey fiber and shot rocks or clay balls at the enemy.

These drawings from the Codex Mendoza show warriors of various ranks taking prisoners by grabbing their buns.
https://commons.wikimedia.org/wiki/File:Codex_Mendoza_folio_65r-3.jpg

To protect themselves from flying rocks, spears, and arrows, the Maya, Aztecs, and other soldiers of ancient Mexico carried wood or wicker shields, which the Aztecs called *Chīmalli*. They were brightly painted in geometric designs, with colorful feathers hanging down. The Maya and Aztecs wore quilted cotton armor, about one-half to one inch thick, which was soaked in brine to form a stiff surface.

The Aztecs believed that when they sacrificed humans, the energy released from the slain victims fed the gods. In return, the gods provided rain, power, protection, and other benefits. In the decades before the Spaniards arrived, the Aztec Empire was unraveling at the edges, with disgruntled populations rising up. When they faced conflict, drought, or other challenges, the Aztecs ramped up the human sacrifices, killing up to twenty thousand people annually. Some scholars believe the number was much higher, perhaps up to a quarter million, but that rate would have quickly wiped ancient Mexico's population out.

With over one thousand sacrifices a month, the Aztecs desperately needed victims. They mostly sacrificed prisoners of war; however, once they conquered the surrounding regions, they no longer had thousands of prisoners to feed the gods. In their minds, failure to sacrifice to the gods would lead to apocalyptic disasters like epidemics, hurricanes, starvation, and invasion by their enemies.

So, they devised ritual warfare called Flower Wars, where the objective was not to kill or conquer but to capture prisoners to sacrifice. The Tlaxcalan people, who lived west of the Aztec heartland, were often the opponents in the Flower Wars, along with the city of Cholula to the south. In a Flower War, the battle ended when both sides captured their quota of sacrificial victims. The Aztecs' perceived need for human sacrifice was so horrific that they staged these battles every twenty days. Of course, it meant losing their own warriors to the opposing side.

Illustration from the Durán Codex of a Flower War against Huexotzinco in Puebla that did not end well for the Aztecs (on the right side of the painting).
https://commons.wikimedia.org/wiki/File:La_derrota_en_la_batalla_de_Atlixco_contra_los_Huejotzingas,_en_el_folio_168v.png

One humorous battle was a fake confrontation to settle the Triple Alliance's leadership question. The original 1428 agreement was for the kings of Tenochtitlan, Texcoco, and Tlacopan to take turns leading the empire. However, when the Mexica-Aztec Moctezuma I became king of Tenochtitlan in 1440, he demanded the other two cities recognize him as supreme emperor (*huey tlatoani*).

To save face, King Nezahualcoyotl of Texcoco proposed a choreographed "battle" to cede ascendency to Tenochtitlan. The warriors from Texcoco lined up facing the Mexica from Tenochtitlan, and each side yelled taunts at the other. The Texcoco warriors abruptly spun around and dashed back to their city with the Mexica in hot pursuit. The battle ended without bloodshed when Nezahualcoyotl lit a gigantic bonfire on Texcoco's highest pyramid in "surrender." From that point on, the Tenochtitlan king ruled the Aztec Empire.

In 1478, the Aztecs suffered a humiliating defeat to the Pacific-Coast Purépecha-Tarascan Empire, located northwest of the Aztec Empire. Despite decades of warfare, the Aztecs could never defeat the Purépecha. King Axayacatl marched with thirty-two thousand Aztec warriors to Taximaroa (today's Hidalgo). But the Purépecha met him with fifty thousand soldiers armed with copper shields and spearheads. The Aztecs' wooden or wicker shields were no match for metal spearheads, and the Purépecha spears were too long for the Aztec warriors to get within striking range with their war clubs. Outnumbered and with inferior weaponry, the Aztecs lost twenty thousand men in one day.

Before this battle, the Aztecs and Purépecha had built garrisons along their borders to discourage attempts to cross into the other's territory. After defeating the Aztecs, the Purépecha increased their fortifications and also took advantage of the Otomi people, who had lost their homeland to the Aztecs. The Otomi people were fierce fighters and among the original inhabitants of the Valley of Mexico. They had formed part of Teotihuacan's multiethnic population in the Classic era, and when that city collapsed, they built their island city of Xaltocan. They lost a brutal war and their island kingdom to the Tepanec-Aztecs in 1395 and migrated south and west to Hidalgo, Puebla, and Tlaxcala.

The Purépecha invited the Otomi to settle in their territory along the Aztec border. All they needed to do was help defend against Aztec incursions. The Otomi were willing to fight their bitter rivals and were grateful for land to settle. After beating the Aztec invasion in 1478, the Purépecha marched southeast later that year in a counterattack, coming within fifty miles of Tenochtitlan. To prevent further catastrophe, the Aztecs negotiated a demilitarized zone between the two empires, and a ceasefire ensued for over three decades.

In 1516, the Aztecs captured Tlahuicole, a legendary Tlaxcalan war hero, the most vicious fighter among his people. The Aztec emperor, Moctezuma II, was so awed by Tlahuicole's gutsiness and prowess that he offered the Tlaxcalan captive his freedom. But Tlahuicole refused, feeling it would be humiliating to return home after being captured. He demanded the usual captive warrior's death of human sacrifice. Instead,

Moctezuma made him commander-in-chief of the Aztec warriors and sent him to fight the Purépecha, who had invaded again.

After Tlahuicole crushed the Purépecha army and returned with hundreds of captives, Moctezuma again offered him freedom or a permanent army command. Once again, Tlahuicole refused, feeling that release was dishonorable and fighting for the enemy was treason, especially since he would have to fight his own people. So, Moctezuma chained him to a huge stone disk called a *temalacatl* in a human sacrificial ritual where two captive warriors fought to the death. Tlahuicole killed the first eight elite warriors who battled him one-on-one but finally fell to the ninth contestant.

In addition to garrisons and using the Otomi people in a buffer zone, the Purépecha maintained cordial relations with their tributary cities on their borders. While the Aztecs demanded oppressive tribute from the city-states they conquered, the Purépecha exchanged resources for tribute. It was more of an equal trade situation that didn't bleed their conquered territories dry. The Purépecha ruled fairly and harmoniously, encouraging loyalty from their far-flung provinces and the willingness to fight against common enemies.

By contrast, the Aztecs ruled their conquered territories harshly, demanding not only commodities as tribute payments but also people. They drafted men for the military and enslaved the children. They frequently raided their unconquered neighbors for sacrificial victims, believing they needed to increase their gory rituals to maintain power. This cruelty cultivated hatred in the surrounding territories, ultimately leading to the Aztec defeat when the Spanish arrived, as several tribes allied with the Europeans.

Key Takeaways:
- Birth ritual for boys with shield and arrow
- Prominent warrior societies based on how many captives were taken in battle
    - Tlamani, Cuextecatl, and Butterfly Warriors
    - Eagle and Jaguar warriors
    - Otomi and Shorn Ones, the highest-ranking warriors
- Ambassadors invited cities to join the Aztec Empire and warned against refusing
    - Relay runners carried messages at high speed

- Spies disguised themselves to fit in and gather information
  - Weaponry: war clubs, spears, dart-throwers, bows and arrows
  - Flower Wars for sacrificial victims
  - Important battles
  - A fake battle to cede supremacy to Tenochtitlan's dominance
  - A decisive struggle lost against the Purépecha, who had metal spearheads and shields
  - The capture of the mighty warrior Tlahuicole of Tlaxcala
- Fortifications: garrisons, demilitarized zone, settling allies on border

Chapter 11: The Spanish Conquest and Its Aftermath

On March 4th, 1517, Francisco Hernández de Córdoba sighted the northern tip of the Yucatán Peninsula after a storm blew his three ships off course on their expedition from Cuba. Sailing along the coast, he was astonished to see the tall and elaborate buildings of a Maya city; the Spaniards had yet to encounter such sophisticated architecture in the New World. The pyramid reminded the conquistadors of Egypt, so they dubbed the city "El Gran Cairo."

The Maya feigned friendliness as they paddled their canoes up to the ships. But when the Spaniards came ashore the next day, the Maya attacked, killing two of their men. Rowing quickly back to their ships, the Spaniards set sail, traveling along the coast, searching for a river or stream as they were desperate for drinking water. But the rivers of the northern Yucatán run underground.

After three weeks, they finally spotted a river, but their landing was disastrous. The Maya attacked, killing over half their men and wounding the rest, with twelve arrows piercing Córdoba's body. He clung to life on the voyage back to Cuba but died on arrival. Yet Governor Velázquez of Cuba was intrigued by the tales of an advanced civilization and people draped in gold and jade ornaments.

Two years later, eleven more ships arrived at Cozumel in the Yucatán, this time commanded by Hernán Cortés. Through sign language, the Maya communicated that two Spaniards had lived nearby for eight years after being shipwrecked. One was Jerónimo de Aguilar, a Franciscan friar, who gratefully joined Cortés as a translator, having learned the Mayan language. The other, a sailor named Gonzalo Guerrero, was covered with piercings and tattoos and had married a Maya noblewoman. He had achieved a high status with his fighting skills, and he was happy to continue in his new life.

Cortés sailed north to Tabasco, where twelve thousand Potonchán-Maya attacked twice, but the Spaniards had cannons, crossbows, muskets, and steel armor and swords. What really terrified the Maya were the horses, which they had never seen before. The Potonchán surrendered with gifts of gold and twenty slave women. One woman, Doña Marina or La Malinche, was an Aztec who had been captured or purchased as a child. She could speak both the Mayan language and the Aztec Nahuatl. Cortés made her one of his translators and his mistress.

A few days later, Moctezuma II stood in his palace in Tenochtitlan, his brow furling at the news that the men with shining armor were building a village at Veracruz. He called several ambassadors, telling them, "Go greet these strangers and give them gifts. Give them gold! The Maya say they like gold. But tell them to stay on the coast. Warn them to stay away from Tenochtitlan! And paint pictures of these strangers and their armor and weapons. Bring those back to me."

The ambassadors greeted Cortés with figurines of gold, and he gave them glass beads and a helmet, which he asked them to bring back filled with gold dust. The ambassadors returned a few days later with the gold dust and polite greetings from Moctezuma. But they repeated Moctezuma's strict warnings to remain on the coast and not to come to Tenochtitlan. Yet the gold was like a siren's call, and Cortés promptly marched inland with his men, horses, fifteen cannons, and translators.

Twenty-five miles from Veracruz, they received a warm welcome from the Totonac people, who assured them they would fight against the Aztecs. But when Cortés reached Tlaxcala, the fierce warriors fought him for three days. Cortés won them over by returning his Tlaxcalan prisoners of war each day instead of sacrificing them as the Aztecs and Tlaxcalans did. His translators instructed the released prisoners to tell the Tlaxcalan chiefs he wished to ally with them against the Aztecs. This was an offer the Tlaxcalans couldn't refuse, so they joined Cortés's entourage.

The Spaniards and Tlaxcalans marched along to Cholula, a long-time ally of Tlaxcala. But the Aztecs had conquered Cholula two years earlier, forcing them to break their alliance with the Tlaxcalans. When Cortés entered the city, everyone was on edge. Bernal Díaz, one of the conquistadors, wrote they found wooden cages "full of men and boys who were being fattened for the sacrifice at which their flesh would be eaten."[37] The Tlaxcalans warned Cortés the warriors of Cholula might attack.

The Cholula people were trying to decide whether to obey Moctezuma's orders to kill the Spaniards or ally with the Spaniards and their old friends, the Tlaxcalans. Doña Marina overheard the local women discussing a planned attack on the Spaniards while they slept, spurring Cortés to launch a preemptive strike. The Spaniards slaughtered three thousand Cholula warriors and nobility in three hours and burned the ancient city.

On November 8th, 1519, Cortés boldly marched across the causeway leading over Lake Texcoco to the island city of Tenochtitlan. Cortés looked around in awe at the resplendent city of 200,000 people. As Tenochtitlan's people looked on, Moctezuma met him on the causeway, regally attired in gold, jewels, and feathers. It was the one-reed year, and whispers swept through the crowd, "Could this be Cē Ācatl Topiltzin Quetzalcoatl? Is the great Toltec king returning as he prophesized he would in a one-reed year?"

With Doña Marina translating, Cortés meets Moctezuma II in this Tlaxcalan illustration from the Lienzo de Tlaxcala Codex.
https://commons.wikimedia.org/wiki/File:Cortez_%26_La_Malinche.jpg

---

[37]Bernal Díaz del Castillo, *The Conquest of New Spain*, trans. J. M. Cohen (Harmondsworth, England: Penguin Books, 1963 [1632]), 150.

Moctezuma greeted Cortés by placing a chain of gold and a garland of flowers around his neck and hosting Cortés and his officers in the palace of Axayacatl, who was his deceased father. But a week later, Cortés learned that the Aztecs had attacked the men he'd left behind in Veracruz. He swept into Moctezuma's palace with several captains, hissing, "Come with us now! If you call for help, we'll run you through."

He hustled Moctezuma into Axayacatl's palace, where Moctezuma lived under house arrest until his death. The Tenochtitlan Aztecs were unnerved by the move and by the Tlaxcalans roaming their city. The city's restlessness continued for five months until Cortés learned that 19 Spanish warships had arrived with 1,400 soldiers. Governor Velázquez of Cuba had commanded Cortés only to explore Mexico, not establish a colony. But Cortés had founded a settlement in Veracruz, so the governor sent men to arrest him.

Appointing his officer Pedro de Alvarado to take charge in Tenochtitlan, Cortés rushed back to the coast, snuck into the camp by night, and captured the Spanish commander. He then set to work wooing the rest of the Spanish forces. "Come back to Tenochtitlan with me! There are storerooms full of gold there. You'll be richer than your wildest dreams."

The newly arrived conquistadors switched sides and marched with Cortés back to Tenochtitlan with ninety-six horses. Two thousand more Tlaxcalans joined them on the way back. Meanwhile, murder and mayhem rocked Tenochtitlan. In Cortés's absence, King Moctezuma had requested and received permission from Alvarado for the nobility to celebrate a beloved Aztec festival. One thousand Aztec aristocrats gathered in the courtyard of the city's ritual center, dancing and singing as drums played.

Suddenly, Alvarado and the Spanish soldiers charged into the courtyard and blocked the exits. They began brutally slaying the revelers, stripping them of any valuables in what is known as the Massacre in the Great Temple. Frantically, the Aztec nobles rushed to find a way out. Some managed to scale the high wall, yelling to the people in the city to come and defend them. A hail of javelins sailed toward the Spaniards, who hurried back to the palace, where the Aztecs blockaded them.

Cortés arrived to find that the Aztecs had made Moctezuma's brother, Cuitláhuac, the new emperor while Moctezuma was still under house arrest. The Aztecs permitted Cortés and his new army to pass through the city, but Cortés knew that fighting could break out at any moment. He ordered Moctezuma to go out on the balcony, calm the people down, and tell them to grant safe passage for the Spaniards out of the city and back to the coast. But the Aztecs considered Moctezuma a puppet for the Spaniards and jeered, flinging rocks and darts at the balcony.

What happened next depended on who was telling the story. The conquistadors reported that three stones struck Moctezuma, and he sustained a head wound and died three days later. However, the Aztecs accused the Spaniards of strangling the emperor. At any rate, the Aztecs already had a new emperor, and Moctezuma was no longer useful to anyone. The crucial matter for the Aztecs was what to do about the Spaniards holed up in the palace of Axayacatl.

Their supplies of gunpowder, food, and water were running out, so Cortés negotiated a one-week ceasefire, telling the Aztecs, "We will return the gold and other treasures we took and leave your city in peace."

Instead, Cortés and his men snuck out of the city that night, hauling as much gold and other treasure as possible. But the causeway connecting the city to the mainland had gaps with portable bridges that the Aztecs removed each night to safeguard the city. The Spaniards brought one movable bridge with them but didn't think about how hundreds of soldiers would need to cross one span before they could move the bridge to the next gap.

It was pouring rain, which kept the Aztecs inside, and no one noticed the men surreptitiously moving through the city. The Spaniards got out to the causeway and crossed the first gap with their movable bridge when an Aztec priest at the peak of the great pyramid sounded the alarm. The Spaniards' portable bridge became stuck, trapping them on the causeway.

Cortés and the cavalry charged ahead down the causeway, with their steeds leaping over the gaps, unaware of the chaos behind them. They reached the shore and whirled their mounts to see a ghastly scene unfolding. The Aztec warriors charged out of the city, sending a hail of arrows toward the soldiers on the causeway. Hundreds of canoes poured out of the city's canals and attacked the Spaniards and Tlaxcalans from the water. The Spaniards who fell into the water were weighed down by the gold they were carrying and drowned.

The Spaniards flee the Aztecs on La Noche Triste or Sad Night. Florentine Codex drawings by Fray Bernardino de Sahagún.
https://commons.wikimedia.org/wiki/File:Spanish_Conquistadors_in_retreat_from_Aztec_Warriors_after_La_Noche_Triste.jpg

Cortés raced back to the causeway to help fight and was wounded in the head. The men got the portable bridge loose, and the survivors finally reached the mainland. On La Noche Triste, or Sad Night, about one thousand Spaniards and two thousand Tlaxcalans perished. They lost all of their artillery and gold, and most of the men were wounded. In a series of letters Cortés wrote to King Charles V, he recorded the horror of the fateful night and the events before and after.[38]

The conquistadors had no time to grieve their lost comrades or tend to their wounds, as thousands of angry Aztecs were closing in. The Tlaxcalans led them north around the connected lakes as they fought off attacks from bands of Aztecs. When the Aztecs killed one of their horses, the Spaniards were so hungry they ate the entire animal, including its skin. About forty thousand Aztecs launched a full-scale attack when they reached Otumba on the northeastern side of the lake system.

Two tactics saved the Spaniards that day. The Castilian cavalry put their horsemanship skills into play, charging the Aztecs, who had never battled horses, and breaking through their lines repeatedly. Cortés told his men to focus their attacks on the Aztec chiefs. After killing the Aztec commander-in-chief, the Aztecs fell back, and the Spaniards and Tlaxcalans chased

---

[38] Hernán Cortés, *Cartas y Relaciones de Hernán Cortés al Emperador Carlos V*, ed. Pascual de Gayangos (Paris: A. Chaix, 1866). https://www.cervantesvirtual.com/nd/ark:/59851/bmc0974782

them off. It was a bittersweet victory. Only 440 Spanish soldiers survived, and all of them were wounded, as were many of the Tlaxcalans.

The soldiers finally stumbled into safety in the mountainous Tlaxcalan territory, and Cortés renewed the terms of an alliance with the Tlaxcalans. He awarded them the city of Cholula, freedom from tribute, and an equal share of the loot from their future forays together. His Veracruz settlement sent reinforcements, and supply ships with more soldiers and horses arrived from Cuba and Spain. Neither of these places realized Cortés was still in power.

Cortés worked his way around the eastern side of Lake Texcoco, solidifying alliances with the Acolhua-Aztecs, the Tepanec-Aztecs, the Otomi, and other tribes against the Mexica-Aztecs. In September 1520, smallpox struck Tenochtitlan, decimating the number of warriors and killing the new emperor, Cuitláhuac. His cousin, Cuauhtémoc, succeeded him as the last Aztec emperor.

Cortés's ingenious battle plan for attacking the island city of Tenochtitlan was to build thirteen small, shallow ships called brigantines, which were propelled by oars and sails and armed with cannons. Using the expertise of Martín López, a carpenter in his entourage with shipbuilding experience, and eight thousand indigenous workers to cut timber, the shipbuilding began. North America's first shipyard was miles from the lake, 7,500 feet above sea level, and in Tlaxcalan territory, where it would be safe from Aztec intrusion. They built a secret canal to the lake and hauled unassembled sections of the ships a mile down to the channel, where they put the ships together and launched them. The Spaniards and Tlaxcalans carried out this impressive feat in only fifty days.[39]

On April 28th, 1521, the ships sailed down the canal and into the lake. At this point, the Spaniards had eighty-six cavalrymen, about one thousand infantrymen, and about twenty thousand indigenous allies fighting with them. One battalion marched to the island of Chapultepec to cut the aqueduct that piped fresh water into Tenochtitlan, which was surrounded by brackish water. From the Chapultepec hilltop, the Spaniards cheered as they watched the ships navigating across the lake to the city of Iztapalapa on the other end of the causeway leading to Tenochtitlan.

---

[39] Robert F. Carter, "North America's First Shipyard," *The Military Engineer* 57, no. 379 (1965): 338–40. http://www.jstor.org/stable/44571688.

Five hundred canoes poured out of Tenochtitlan but stopped short when they drew close to the ships. While the Aztecs silently floated, scrutinizing the vessels, the wind arose, and Cortés ordered the ships to attack. With the wind behind their sails, the brigantines cut through the water toward the canoes, crushing any that did not move fast enough. The Spanish land army rushed down the causeway while the brigantines prevented the Aztec canoes from getting closer. When Aztecs from other cities launched a rear attack, ten thousand Tlaxcalans blocked their way.

The brigantines attacked by water and the land army from the causeways.
Fray Bernardino de Sahagún, Florentine Codex.
https://commons.wikimedia.org/wiki/File:Brigantines_in_the_Siege_of_Tenochtitlan.jpg

The Spaniards had complete control of the causeways, but rooftop archers in the city prevented them from getting close. The brigantines and foot soldiers launched cannon fire and shot fiery arrows to burn and destroy the structures on the city's perimeter. The small ships even sailed into the canals interlacing the metropolis, firing cannonballs along the way. Cortés's land forces reached the city's center and set fire to the temple complex.

But the sun was setting, so the Spaniards retreated to the causeway for the night. The Mexica-Aztecs used this moment to counterattack from the rear, killing more than a thousand Tlaxcalans and capturing some Spaniards. They hauled these men to the top of the highest pyramid and cut their beating hearts out of their chests.

The Spaniards set up camp on the causeways, and months of fighting ensued. The Spaniards gradually gained control of sections of the city and burned those neighborhoods down, forcing the population into an ever-dwindling remnant of the city. At first, the Aztecs outside the city smuggled in water and food by canoe, but the brigantines ended that. With the aquifer cut off, the city had no fresh water, and the people began drinking the saline water in the canals, dying from dysentery and dehydration as a result. Most other Aztec cities around the lake surrendered.

Finally, thousands of men, women, and children spilled out of the one-eighth section of the city still standing. Despite their surrender, the Tlaxcalans immediately attacked against Cortés's orders, killing over fifteen thousand citizens. Then, a fleet of canoes launched into the lake, which the Spanish brigantines intercepted. In one canoe, they saw the emperor, Cuauhtémoc, with his family. They captured him on August 13th, 1521, ending the siege. The Aztec Empire had fallen.

Most of the other civilizations in Mexico surrendered within a year with little or no fighting, hoping to avoid the devastation visited on the Aztecs. The Maya continued fighting fiercely; it took 170 years for the Spaniards to conquer all the Maya city-states. Despite eleven years of warfare, northwestern Mexico's fierce, nomadic Chichimeca remained undefeated. Finally, the Spanish friars demanded an end to the gory warfare and instituted a new program of colonizing Christianized Tlaxcalans in northwestern Mexico. They befriended the nomadic Chichimeca and helped "tame" them, teaching the Chichimeca to be ranchers and farmers. Spanish friars lived among them, introducing the Chichimeca to Catholicism.

Key Takeaways:
- 1517: Francisco Hernández de Córdoba discovers Mexico
- 1519: Hernán Cortés arrives and heads inland
    - Acquired Fray Jerónimo de Aguilar and Doña Marina (La Malinche) as translators
    - Allied with the Totonacs and Tlaxcalans
    - Destroyed Cholula
- Arrival in Tenochtitlan
    - Placed Moctezuma II under house arrest
    - Massacre of noblemen in the temple
    - Moctezuma killed
- La Noche Triste
    - Spaniards attempted to sneak out of Tenochtitlan
    - Aztecs killed or wounded most Spaniards and many Tlaxcalans
- Cortés regrouped and planned siege
    - Formed alliances with many cities
    - Built small ships and a canal to Lake Texcoco
    - Smallpox hit Tenochtitlan
- Siege of Tenochtitlan
    - Spaniards attacked by ships and land army
    - Tenochtitlan fell after five months; the emperor captured
- Aftermath
    - Most civilizations in Mexico surrendered with little resistance
    - Maya fought for 170 years
    - Chichimeca undefeated; enticed to join a settlement program

PART FOUR:
An Unforgettable Legacy

Chapter 12: Legendary Figures

The history of ancient Mexico is the stories of its people, from the farmers in the fields to the rulers in the palaces. We have little surviving information for most of its people other than what can be gleaned from archaeological analysis. But the tales of some legendary figures have been preserved through oral traditions and written accounts. Let's take a look at some of them.

Itzamná and Kukulkan

Zamná (or Kukulkan) was a priest who legend says arrived in the Yucatán from Tula. He founded (or renovated) Chichén Itzá and other cities in the Yucatán and invented writing. For his contributions to civilization, he became Itzamná, the god of the sky, one of the most prominent deities of the Maya. The paradox is that the Maya believed the god Itzamná created the world from chaos and created human beings, so how could Zamná become Itzamná if humans already existed? Not to mention the Maya had been writing for centuries before Tula was founded (which did not have an advanced writing system). Apparently, both a god and a person had the same name, and their stories got mixed up. Some scholars believe that Zamná was Cē Ācatl Topiltzin since he came from the Toltec city of Tula.

The deity Itzamná and his wife, the moon goddess Ixchel, were the parents of the other gods. From Itzamná flowed the sky and earth, day and night, sun and moon, birth and death, male and female, and the heavens and the underworld. Itzamná invented the sciences, astrology, medicine, agriculture, the calendar, and writing and taught them to the

Maya. His images are often of a stern older man sitting on a throne with a long, pointed nose. He is sometimes portrayed as a crocodile or as the Bird of Heaven (Itzam Yeh) perched on the World Tree (Ceiba), holding a two-headed snake in its beak.

Itzamná, Maya creation god.
Salvador alc, CC BY-SA 3.0 <https://creativecommons.org/licenses/by-sa/3.0>, via Wikimedia Commons; https://commons.wikimedia.org/wiki/File:Itzamna_sculpture.JPG

Sometimes, Itzamná is equated with Kukulkan, the feathered serpent deity, who is part rattlesnake and part quetzal bird. The Olmecs, Teotihuacanos, Zapotecs, Mixtecs, Toltecs, and Aztecs also worshiped the Feathered Serpent as the creator god of the sky and bringer of the wind and rain. The Toltecs and Aztecs knew him as Quetzalcoatl, the god of agriculture, arts, and science and the inventor of the calendar. He gifted corn to humans and was associated with Venus, the morning star.

Spearthrower Owl (Atlatl Cauac or Jatz'om Kuy)

The Teotihuacanos did not keep records of their monarchs, but Mayan inscriptions named Spearthrower Owl as king of Teotihuacan from 374 to 439 CE. His reign coincided with an uprising when Teotihuacan's Feathered Serpent Temple was burned and partly obscured by the construction of the Adosada platform. Why would the Maya of Tikal in Guatemala write about the king of Teotihuacan, who was located almost eight hundred miles northwest? The inscriptions say that a warlord of Spearthrower Owl, called Siyaj K'ak' (Fire-is-Born), invaded Tikal in 378 CE, killing the Maya king Jaguar Paw (Chak Tok Ich'aak I). General Fire-is-Born made Spearthrower Owl's son, First Crocodile (Yax Nuun Ayiin), the new king of Tikal.[40]

The Maya said that General Fire-is-Born went on to conquer Uaxactun, just south of Tikal, and he and his descendants ruled that city for generations. First Crocodile ruled Tikal until he died in 404 and was succeeded by his son Storm Sky (Sihyaj Chan K'awiil), who ruled for fifty-two years until his death in 456. Teotihuacan also installed Great Sun, Quetzal Bird the First (K'inich Yax K'uk' Mo') as the king of Copan, over two hundred miles south of Tikal in Honduras.

Curiously, First Crocodile might not have been the Teotihuacan prince the Maya believed him to be. A pyramid in Tikal supposedly houses his tomb, as an inscription on a cup beside his skeleton reads, "The cup of Spearthrower Owl's son." But isotype analysis of the remains, which shows the person's lifelong diet, indicates he grew up around Tikal. He might have been passing himself off as Teotihuacan royalty, or perhaps he was a Teotihuacan prince who grew up in the Yucatán for some reason.

Nezahualcoyotl

Nezahualcoyotl (1402–1472 CE) was king of Texcoco after masterminding and commanding the coalition army that brought the Aztec Empire into being. He was a poet, prophet, and engineer, and after the Triple Alliance was established, he ruled the Alcoa-Aztecs. However, before that happened, when he was still a teenage prince, he fled to the mountainous Tlaxcala territory after the invading Tepanecs killed his father. While in exile, he experienced a sudden spiritual perception, which was written down by his great-grandson:

---

[40] Michael D. Coe, *The Maya (Ancient Peoples and Places Series)* (London and New York: Thames & Hudson, 1999), 90.

"Some immensely powerful and unknown god is the creator of the whole universe. He is the only one that can console me in my affliction and help me in such anguish as my heart feels; I want him to be my helper and protection."[41]

Nezahualcoyotl's painting in the Codex Ixtlilxóchitl.
https://commons.wikimedia.org/wiki/File:Nezahualcoyotl.jpg

Once he trounced the Tepanecs and became king of Texcoco, Nezahualcoyotl built a pyramid to Tloque Nahuaque, "the unknown yet always near, self-existing creator."[42] Tloque Nahuaque was unusual in that he did not require human sacrifice. Nezahualcoyotl only offered incense and flowers to his god.

Nezahualcoyotl had 110 children with his wives and concubines, yet he fell in love with the wife of a minor king under him. He sent that king to fight the Tlaxcalans, where he was killed, and Nezahualcoyotl then made the beautiful Queen Azcalxochitzin his wife. Soon after, swarms of locusts

---

[41] Juan Bautista de Pomar. "Relación de Tezcoco," in *Relaciones de la Nueva España*, ed. Vázquez Chamorro. (Madrid: Historia 16, 1991).

[42] Pomar, "Relación de Tezcoco."

struck Texcoco, stripping the fields bare of corn, tomatoes, and peppers. The crops that survived shriveled from drought. Nezahualcoyotl's people were starving, and he felt his sin had caused the famine. He opened the treasury to buy food for his citizens and paid the school fees of children who had lost their parents in the disaster.

Xicotencatl the Elder

Xicotencatl was the long-lived Tlaxcalan ruler of Tizatlan who cautioned the Council of Tlaxcala when considering Cortés's proposed alliance. In the debate over whether to join forces with the Spaniards, a Tlaxcalan noble named Maxixcatzin encouraged the coalition. He said the gods and ancestors ordained this opportunity to break the Aztec yoke.

Xicotencatl the Elder in the Lienzo de Tlaxcala Codex.
https://commons.wikimedia.org/wiki/File:Xicotencatl_the_elder.jpg

Yet Xicotencatl warned, "Cortés might be our friend now, but would he still be once Tenochtitlan falls? Would he become the enemy within? Are the Spaniards gods? Or are they ravenous monsters gorging themselves on gold? Would we spill our blood only to become enslaved to them?"

Although the aged Xicotencatl pointed out that defeating the Mexica-Aztecs would come at a price, the Council of Tlaxcala voted to ally with Cortés. The Lienzo de Tlaxcala Codex says that Xicotencatl was 120 years old and had over five hundred wives and children when he first met Cortés.

Apoxpalon (Paxbolonacha)

Apoxpalon was a Chontal Maya of Tabasco, a group that claimed lineage from the Olmecs. In 1525 CE, he rose from the position of merchant to become king of Itzamkanac, the capital of the Chontal Maya city-state. These Maya didn't have royal dynasties but elected their kings based on their abilities, usually merchants who acquired a knowledge base through their travels. Apoxpalon's specific abilities included an astute understanding of arithmetic, and he had broad experience in farming, fishing, and hunting.

Apoxpalon became king shortly after Cortés crushed the Aztec Empire and was nervous about what would happen to him when Cortés traveled to his region. His son met Cortés with gifts of gold, telling him that his father had died. Cortés expressed his sympathy but suspected it was all subterfuge, as he knew King Apoxpalon had been alive just four days before. Nevertheless, Cortés gave the young prince the bead necklace he was wearing as a gift and continued on his way.

Cortés arrived in Teoticaccac, about eighteen miles from Itzamkanac, where the city's leader graciously welcomed him. Teoticaccac's ruler disclosed that Apoxpalon was alive and well but afraid that Cortés would kill him and take his wealth. Cortés then interrogated Apoxpalon's son, who admitted his father was alive. Two days later, Apoxpalon arrived, apologetically explaining his fear of foreigners and horses. He invited Cortés to Itzamkanac, where the Spaniards stayed in his palace and enjoyed a night of feasting and celebration. When Cortés left the next day, he gave the king a horse as a gift, and Apoxpalon overcame his fear of the animal and learned how to ride[43]

Hernán Cortés

Hernán Cortés's overriding ambition and charismatic personality launched a stellar career, yet his disregard for authority and ruthlessness sometimes derailed his goals. In his mid-twenties, he caught the eye of Cuba's governor, Diego Velázquez, who elevated him in rank. Yet the governor was displeased when Cortés became romantically involved with Velázquez's sister-in-law Catalina while flirting with her sister. Cortés married Catalina mainly to further his career.

---

[43] Susan Schroeder, ed., *Chimalpahin's Conquest: A Nahua Historian's Rewriting of Francisco Lopez de Gomara's La conquista de Mexico* (Redwood City: Stanford University Press, 2010), 386-9. https://doi.org/10.1515/9780804775069-184

In 1518, Velázquez commissioned Cortés to lead an expedition to Mexico but changed his mind at the last minute. Cortés set sail anyway, an act of mutiny, which was then exacerbated by Cortés establishing a colony in Veracruz against the governor's strict orders. He declared himself independent of Cuba and presented his new town as a colony of Charles V, King of Spain and the Holy Roman Emperor. Cortés sent a ship full of gold with letters to Charles, telling him about his explorations and why he had separated from Velázquez.

Once Cortés conquered Tenochtitlan, he eliminated indigenous leaders he considered a threat by accusing them of conspiracy and hanging them. He did this with Xicotencatl the Elder's son, fulfilling the ancient leader's prophecy. Cortés allowed the last Aztec emperor, Cuauhtémoc, to live for four years but then took him on an expedition into Maya territory and hanged him for alleged conspiracy. To rein in Cortés and other conquistadors, King Charles established the Council of the Indies to govern all of Spain's new colonies in the Americas and the Pacific.

Hernán Cortés, Naval Museum of Madrid.
https://commons.wikimedia.org/wiki/File:Hern%C3%A1n_Cort%C3%A9s_an%C3%B3nimo.jpg

A year after Tenochtitlan fell, Catalina came to Mexico, unhappy to find her husband's pregnant translator and mistress, Doña Marina, living in his palace. At a dinner party, she lashed out at Cortés and then stormed out of the room. Hours later, she was found dead in her room. Cortés was charged with murder by strangulation, but the charges were dropped, perhaps due to lavish bribes. He acknowledged Doña Marina's son, Martín, as his own, eventually making him legitimate.

In 1529, Cortés married Doña Juana de Zúñiga, a Spanish noblewoman, and Charles V made him marquess of the Valley of Oaxaca. A year earlier, Cortés violated Moctezuma II's daughter Doña Isabel and got her pregnant. At around age twelve, Isabel became the child bride of her uncle Cuitláhuac, who became emperor after Cortés put her father under house arrest. Months later, Cuitláhuac died of smallpox, and she married her cousin Cuauhtémoc, the last Aztec emperor. Cortés executed Cuauhtémoc several years later and took the seventeen-year-old Isabel into his home. When she got pregnant, he quickly married Isabel to a friend, and a baby girl was born several months later. Isabel refused to have anything to do with the infant, so Cortés sent his daughter to a relative to raise.

Cortés accumulated breathtaking wealth through his landholdings, the treasures he acquired in his conquests, and his thirty-five silver mines. Yet he spent most of his money on more expeditions and was heavily in debt when he died of dysentery. However, he did acknowledge and provide for his eleven children from his second wife and multiple mistresses.

Key Takeaways:
- Itzamná and Kukulkan
    - Itzamná was the god of the sky and creation
    - Sometimes equated with Kukulkan, the feathered serpent deity
- Spearthrower Owl
    - According to the Maya, king of Teotihuacan from 374 to 439 CE
    - His general invaded Tikal in 378; his descendants ruled several Maya cities
- Apoxpalon
    - Chontal Maya merchant who became king
    - Faked his death to Cortés
- Nezahualcoyotl
    - King of Texcoco, commander of coalition Aztec army

- - Poet, prophet, engineer, and one of the Triple Alliance founders
  - Worshiped the omniscient, uncreated creator
- Xicotencatl the Elder: aged Tlaxcalan ruler who argued against allying with Spaniards
- Hernán Cortés
  - Extremely ambitious, ruthless, disregarded authority, yet persuasive and charming
  - Began career in Cuba, then conquered much of Mexico and part of Central America

Chapter 13: Art, Architecture, and Artifacts

Palaces, pyramids, brilliant murals, painted pottery, and ornaments of jade and gold all contributed to ancient Mexico's rich assortment of architecture and art. Some themes pervaded the various cultures, but each civilization had distinctive features. The art and architecture of ancient Mexico mirrored the political ideals, religious beliefs, worldviews, and lifestyles of its people. Viewing these artifacts gives us a portrait of what life was like and how people viewed the spiritual and physical worlds.

The Olmecs

In addition to Mesoamerica's first known pyramid and their unique colossal heads, the Olmecs left a legacy of art and architecture that impacted future cultures. Using the Coatzacoalcos River system, they imported jadeite and obsidian from Guatemala, from which they carved weaponry and images of supernatural creatures. Their expansive trade network, which spread from the Gulf Coast to the Pacific Ocean, meant that the Olmecs influenced other civilizations far from their heartland.

Their images featured the were-jaguar, a part-jaguar and part-human creature, perhaps an Olmec deity. These carvings had a cleft head, almond eyes, and a downturned gaping mouth. Most were-jaguar images were babies held out in the arms of a man, as if in sacrifice. The Olmecs also carved jade jaguar masks. Olmec paintings discovered deep within the Juxtlahuaca Cave in Guerrero, dating from 1200 to 900 BCE, depict a leaping jaguar and a feathered serpent. A fascinating image of a bearded man with a tail and spots on his arms and legs appears to be either a half-jaguar and half-man creature or a man wearing a jaguar skin.

The Las Limas figure is a twenty-two-inch-high greenstone carving of a man holding a limp were-jaguar baby, dating from 1000 to 600 BCE.
Mag2017, CC BY-SA 4.0 <https://creativecommons.org/licenses/by-sa/4.0>, via Wikimedia Commons; https://commons.wikimedia.org/wiki/File:Se%C3%B1or_de_las_limas_2.jpg

The Maya

Maya art was partly for visual pleasure, partly to depict historical events, but mainly to express their polytheistic religious beliefs. It featured dragon and serpent motifs as a link between the underworld and the land of the living. Images of deities often had jaguar features, representing courage and strength. They believed their most powerful priests and kings could shapeshift into jaguars; thus, some images have faces that are jaguar on one side and human on the other.

The Maya demonstrated an understanding of chemistry in their brightly colored pigments. They blended clay with indigo leaves, creating a chemical reaction that turned yellow or turquoise, depending on what they added to the mixture. Their murals usually reflected war or religious festivals but occasionally the everyday life of non-royal people. The Maya also carved stone, jade, and wood. They cut enormous boulders into the shape of crocodiles, jaguars, and snakes. Death masks of jade, gold, or shells covered the faces of deceased royalty.

Captive warriors plead for mercy from King Yajaw Chan Muwaan in this mural from Bonampak.
https://commons.wikimedia.org/wiki/File:01-maya-lidar-mapping.jpg

Maya architecture featured a network of causeways spreading from the ceremonial centers, often acting as dams in the lowland cities. They built trios of pyramids, with two smaller pyramids facing a giant one. Sometimes, they had pyramid quads, with three small pyramids across from the larger one, and occasionally, they built identical pyramids side by side. The Maya constructed some cities according to a pattern that reflected certain glyphs when viewed from above.

Maya jade death mask from the city of Calakmul.
Estela Parra, CC BY-SA 4.0 <https://creativecommons.org/licenses/by-sa/4.0>, via Wikimedia Commons; https://commons.wikimedia.org/wiki/File:Mascara_de_calakmul.jpg

The Zapotecs

Some of the Zapotecs' most distinctive artwork revolved around burials. They formed elaborate clay urns, which were buried close to the bodies, representing hybrid bat creatures and jaguars (the Maya and Zapotecs worshiped both animals). The funerary urns also featured various deities sitting cross-legged with elaborate headdresses. Sometimes, they were realistic human figures, perhaps representing the deceased person.

Zapotec tombs for illustrious citizens had cement floors, stone or adobe walls, and a doorway. Once the person was buried, a high mound of dirt covered the vault. The funerary urns were placed in groups of five just outside the tomb, usually on the door lintel. It's a mystery what the hollow urns held, if anything, as no residue remains. Like the Maya and Mixtecs, the Zapotecs carved death masks and were among the first in Mexico to work with metals.

A Zapotec funerary urn from the Classic era.
Simon Burchell, CC BY-SA 3.0 <https://creativecommons.org/licenses/by-sa/3.0>, via Wikimedia Commons; https://commons.wikimedia.org/wiki/File:Zapotec_funerary_urn_1,_Museo_de_Am%C3%A9rica.jpg

One especially intriguing example of Zapotec architecture was the arrowhead-shaped Building J, which was built in Monte Albán around 100 BCE. It pointed to the Capella (or Goat) star, the sixth-brightest star in the sky. The Capella is actually a group of four stars that are exceptionally brilliant when close to the horizon on winter nights. The arrowhead building is dedicated to military conquests, with the heads of conquered kings carved upside-down around the exterior.

Teotihuacan

Archaeologists believe that Teotihuacan was ruled by a council rather than one powerful king for at least part of its existence. The artwork for this multiethnic city doesn't glorify its rulers, only deities and primordial creation mythology. Humans are often depicted wearing similar clothing with no distinguishing characteristics. Art historian Esther Pasztory believed the impersonal repetitive artwork might have been mandated to promote an egalitarian society where collective values trumped individualism.[44]

A Teotihuacan priest wearing a dragon mask.
UNESCO / Dominique Roger, CC BY-SA 3.0 IGO <https://creativecommons.org/licenses/by-sa/3.0/igo/deed.en>, via Wikimedia Commons; https://commons.wikimedia.org/wiki/File:Painting,_Mexico_-_UNESCO_-_PHOTO0000001337_0001.tiff

Brilliant murals in crimson, green, and gold covered the palace and temple walls, as well as the exterior walls of the apartment compounds. They featured priests offering sacrifices, jaguars, and deities like the Feathered Serpent and the Great Goddess (called Spider Woman because of the spiders dangling from her headdress). People are usually depicted with short, squat bodies that are almost eclipsed by enormous masks and headdresses.

---

[44] Esther Pasztory, *Teotihuacan: An Experiment in Living* (Norman: University of Oklahoma Press, 1997), xv-xvi.

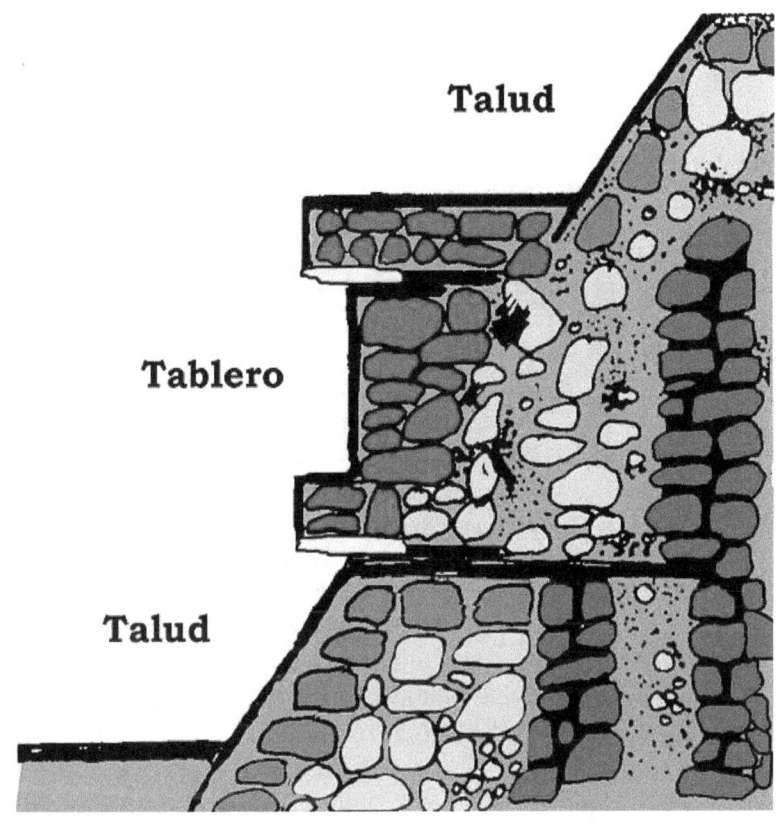

Talud-tablero architecture.
HJPD, CC BY-SA 3.0 <https://creativecommons.org/licenses/by-sa/3.0>, via Wikimedia Commons; https://commons.wikimedia.org/wiki/File:TableroTalud.jpg

At 216 feet, Teotihuacan's Sun Pyramid was the highest in Mexico when it was built and is the seventh-largest pyramid in the world today by volume. The Sun Pyramid and Cholula's Great Pyramid (the largest in the world by volume) were built using the talud-tablero architecture, a Teotihuacan hallmark. Cholula had a close relationship with Teotihuacan, as well as a similar culture. A talud-tablero pyramid has a steep slope (talud) with a ledge sticking out like a table (tablero).

The Mixtecs

The Mixtecs were the premier artisans of Mexico's Postclassic era and were especially renowned for their exquisite gold work. They were masters of elaborate mosaics of turquoise, jade, obsidian, and coral, and their delicate carvings on jaguar bones and wood were highly prized throughout Mexico. Their codices or complex pictorial stories written on deerskin were far more detailed and stylistic than those of the Maya or Aztecs.

An intricate Mixtec golden serpent labret (lip plug) ornament.
*Sailko, CC BY 3.0 <https://creativecommons.org/licenses/by/3.0>, via Wikimedia Commons;
https://commons.wikimedia.org/wiki/File:Messico,_mixtechi-aztechi,_labret_(orecchino_per_sotto_il_labbro_inferiore)_a_forma_di_serpente,_IX-XI_sec,_oro_sbalzato_01.JPG*

Mixtec pottery displayed unparalleled diversity and form, with striking scenes in precise detail. One beautiful example of Mixtec polychrome ceramics is a pedestal bowl with a brightly polished orange and red surface. Three snarling jaguars were painted white, grey, black, and brown. Feather-like blades jut out from a feline's rump and claw, possibly representing obsidian blades used in sacrifice.

A Mixtec ceramic pedestal bowl.
*Metropolitan Museum of Art, CC0, via Wikimedia Commons;
https://commons.wikimedia.org/wiki/File:Pedestal_Bowl_MET_DP102174.jpg*

The Toltecs

The Toltecs' name meant craftsmen, and their fame in stunning architecture and crafted objects especially impressed the Aztecs, who sought to emulate their culture. The Aztecs spent twenty years living and studying the culture when they arrived in Tula, which had become a ghost town. When they left, they took artifacts and returned later to take more. The Toltecs specialized in sculptures, including reliefs, pillars carved in the shape of warriors, and smaller carved pieces.

One type of small sculpture, the chacmool, originated with the Toltecs, who introduced them to the Maya of Chichén Itza. The Aztecs also adopted this art form. The chacmool were small stone statues carved to look like a human man lying on his back propped up on his elbows and balancing a bowl on his chest. The head is turned to the side and looking up. The bowl on the figurine's chest held a sacrificial offering; in the case of the Aztecs, it held a human heart cut from a sacrificial victim. The Toltecs likely used it for the same purpose.

This chacmool is from Chichén Itza, which had a strong Toltec influence.
Luis Alberto Lecuna/Melograna, CC BY-SA 2.0 <https://creativecommons.org/licenses/by-sa/2.0>,
via Wikimedia Commons;
https://commons.wikimedia.org/wiki/File:Maya_Chac_Mool_by_Luis_Alberto_Melograna.jpg

The Toltecs carved mesmerizing reliefs on walls, such as the "wall of serpents" in Tula, which was over one hundred feet long and depicted human skeletons and slithering snakes. The serpents appear to be eating the human bones, or the skeletons are emerging from their mouths. The skeletons might have represented revered ancestors, especially since the wall is just next to Pyramid B, which was dedicated to the city's rulers. Skeletons, skulls, and human hearts seemed to pervade Toltec culture, with depictions of jaguars and eagles feeding on human hearts and skull racks of sacrificial victims.

The Aztecs

The Aztecs' flashy art and architecture were used as propaganda to exert political and cultural dominance over conquered regions. The Aztec myths depict them as wandering nomads from the northwestern deserts who entered the Valley of Mexico as a cultural blank slate. Descriptions of Aztlán, their mythical island of origin, talk about its natural beauty, not its architecture or art. The Aztec art and architecture were a hodgepodge of influences, mainly from the Toltecs, Teotihuacanos, and Mixtecs. They brought Mixtec and Zapotec artisans into Tenochtitlan and appropriated styles from other Mesoamericans. The city's sculptures, murals, and architecture were an incongruous mixture of styles.

Like the Mixtecs, the Aztecs built libraries of codices or pictorial books about history, religion, and administrative matters, such as tribute payments. They used amate paper made from the Ficus tree, with 480,000 sheets of paper provided as an annual tribute payment from forty towns in the Morelos area. The art in the codices was not as complex as the Mixteca codices, but both had artwork that was more representative than realistic.

The Mixtec artist community in Tenochtitlan produced exquisite pendants, earrings, and other jade, turquoise, amethyst, and gold jewelry. They also created stunning mosaic sculptures, such as a double-headed serpent carved from cedar and covered in "scales" of turquoise with a scarlet mouth and nose from the Spondylus spiny oyster. Its gleaming white fangs were cut from conch shells. The Aztecs had several serpent gods, such as the Fire Serpent, Feathered Serpent, and Cloud Serpent. This sculpture was probably Xiuhcoatl, the Fire Serpent (or Turquoise Snake).

Double-headed serpent turquoise mosaic

British Museum, CC BY-SA 4.0 <https://creativecommons.org/licenses/by-sa/4.0>, via Wikimedia Commons; https://commons.wikimedia.org/wiki/File:Double_headed_turquoise_serpentAztecbritish_museum.jpg

The Aztec nobility and priests loved to drape themselves in featherwork clothing and headdresses. Their favorite feathers were from the emerald green and red quetzal birds of the rainforest. Moctezuma II had a zoo and botanical gardens just outside Tenochtitlan, where flamingos and other brilliantly colored birds produced feathers. Featherwork artisans, who had a designated neighborhood in Tenochtitlan, also created eye-catching mosaics from feather pieces.

Key Takeaways:
- Olmecs: Colossal heads, were-jaguar, jaguar masks, cave paintings
- Maya
    - Bright pigment for paint formed by chemical reaction
    - Architecture: causeways, pyramid grouping, cities portraying glyphs from above
- Zapotecs
    - Elaborate tombs with groups of funerary masks
    - Arrowhead building pointing to the Capella star
- Teotihuacan
    - Artwork impersonal and repetitive, promoting egalitarianism
    - Talud-tablero architecture in pyramids
- Mixtecs: master goldsmiths renowned for exquisite artistry
- Toltecs: chacmool and wall relief of serpents devouring human skeletons
- Aztecs
    - Appropriated styles from other cultures, especially Toltec and Mixtec
    - Used 480,000 sheets of paper from Morelos for pictorial codices and records
    - Featherwork clothing and mosaics

Chapter 14: Ancient Cities

Spectacular reminders of once-great civilizations cover Mexico's landscape, and lidar technology continues to locate the ruins of grand cities in the southern rainforests. Most of these archaeological sites are still being excavated and analyzed, with intriguing new secrets coming to light. Mexico has a diverse collection of stunning ancient cities, so let's explore several remarkable Maya cities and the multiethnic city of Teotihuacan.

Ek' Balam

One of Mexico's earliest cities, Ek' Balam, was founded about 300 BCE near the top of the Yucatán Peninsula. Its name means Black Jaguar or Jaguar Star. The city had a long history, but it dramatically declined in the Postclassic age. At the height of its power in the late Classic era, it was the capital of the Talol Kingdom, receiving tribute from the surrounding region, with roads leading out in all directions.

The city covered about ten square miles, with defensive walls surrounding over forty structures of temples and elite residences in the city's center. The religious and administrative centers were in two plazas on a north-south axis. Over forty inscriptions were carved or painted on the walls, giving historical information on its rulers in the 8th and 9th centuries. The enormous "Oval Palace" has rounded walls, a unique feature of three Maya cities in the Yucatán Peninsula (the other two are Tulum and Chichén Itza). Since only a fraction of the city has been excavated, new discoveries will shed more light on the city's history.

"Angels" or winged warriors on Ukit Kan Le'k Tok's ornate tomb.
Photo modified: zoomed in. Credit: Dennis Jarvis from Halifax, Canada, CC BY-SA 2.0
<https://creativecommons.org/licenses/by-sa/2.0>, via Wikimedia Commons;
https://commons.wikimedia.org/wiki/File:Mexico-6147_-_Mayan_Angels_-_I_don%27t_think_so..._(4669701256).jpg

Ek' Balam's first king mentioned in inscriptions was Ukit Kan Le'k Tok, who ruled from 770 to 801 CE. He built the extravagant "acropolis," which was 90 feet high and 480 feet long, with stairways leading up its six stories. Within its fourth level is his well-preserved tomb behind an intricate frieze, sitting inside the colossal fangs of a gaping jaguar mouth. The elaborate stucco façade features geometrical motifs and unique angel-like winged warriors. Scholars debate the mystery of these winged men, which are not seen elsewhere in Mesoamerica. What do they represent?

Teotihuacan

A stupendous political and commercial empire, Teotihuacan was established about the same time as Ek' Balam and reached its zenith in the early Classic era. Its stunning ruins captured the imagination of the Aztecs and still amaze tourists today. Teotihuacan was the capital of the entire Valley of Mexico and controlled trade from the Gulf Coast to the Pacific Ocean and well into Central America. Its culture impacted most of central and southern Mexico, with its distinct architecture and artistry seen in Guatemala, Honduras, and Belize.

As a cosmopolitan metropolis with multiple ethnicities housed in over two thousand apartment compounds, Teotihuacan had unparalleled cultural and social diversity. The archaeological record shows that the Gulf Coast people, Maya, Oaxacan, and other immigrants sustained their cultural identity, albeit with some adjustments. The various ethnicities maintained strong links with their homelands, which bolstered Teotihuacan's trade monopoly.

Teotihuacan passed through several phases of religious and political upheaval. No archaeological evidence of human sacrifice exists for its first several centuries, at least not on a large scale or as a state ritual. The first known human sacrifice was at the dedication of the Feathered Serpent Pyramid, where about two hundred people were sacrificed between 150 and 200 CE.

The early layers of the Moon Pyramid did not show human sacrifice, but small numbers of humans were sacrificed during the renovations, which took place around 250 CE. At about the same time, child sacrificial victims were buried under the Sun Pyramid at each level. A large-scale massacre or human sacrifice of Maya immigrants occurred in the central Plaza of Columns around 350 CE. After this, human sacrifice seems to have diminished or ended at the state level, as no further sacrificial victims have been found in the archaeological record.

Teotihuacan pottery warrior.
Gary Todd, CC0, via Wikimedia Commons;
https://commons.wikimedia.org/wiki/File:Teotihuacan_Pottery_Warrior_Figure.jpg

In addition to the three great pyramids lining the main corridor, which the Aztecs called the Avenue of the Dead, the Xalla palace had a large pyramid encircled by four smaller pyramids. The smaller pyramids were dedicated to the rain god, the mountain god, the water goddess, and the fire god. Brilliant murals adorned the palace walls; however, it burned down around 550 CE in the revolt that spelled the beginning of Teotihuacan's collapse.

Chichén Itza

As Teotihuacan declined, the Maya city of Chichén Itza sprang up in the Yucatán Peninsula about forty miles southwest of Ek' Balam. Its variety of architectural styles suggests a multicultural population, similar to Teotihuacan. It might have received migrants from Teotihuacan and Maya cities once they declined in the late Classic era. Its archaeological record and legend of the priest Zamná point to a definite Toltec influence via several waves of immigrants.

Chichén Itza reached its zenith from 900 to 1000 CE as the political capital of the central and northern Yucatán. Its vast trade empire stretched into central Mexico and down to southern Central America via its Isla Cerritos port on the Yucatán's northern coast. Chichén Itza experienced two distinct periods of growth. The first was mainly Maya architecture from 800 to 1000, followed by a partial collapse due to a severe one-hundred-year drought. As rainfall resumed and the Toltecs migrated in, a second wave of construction continued, lasting from 1100 to 1200.

In 1527, Spain attempted to conquer the Yucatán. The Maya brutally defeated and destroyed most Spanish forces in the first campaign. In 1532, the Spaniards tried to gain control of the central Yucatán by defeating Chichén Itza. They were initially successful, but the Maya launched a counterattack within months, driving most Spaniards from the peninsula in 1535. It would take another fifty years for the Spaniards to gain a shaky hold on the Yucatán, and only then because three epidemics had killed half the Maya population.[45]

Xochicalco

Sixty miles southwest of today's Mexico City, Xochicalco rose to power as Teotihuacan faded, growing to a population of about twenty thousand. Although a settlement had existed for centuries, it grew into a city when the Maya Olmeca-Xicalanca from Campeche arrived around 650 CE.

---

[45] Georges Frey, "The Endless Conquest of Yucatán," *Popular Archaeology*, January 14, 2022.

Some Teotihuacanos probably migrated to Xochicalco since its architecture features a Maya and Teotihuacan blend with a bit of Zapotec and Gulf Coast influence.

The Xochicalco people maintained their calendar's accuracy by cutting a hole in a cave in the hillside through which the sun shone directly to the floor twice a year in mid-May and late July. The Pyramid of the Plumed Serpents featured gently sloping talud-tablero walls surrounding an open-air courtyard rather than reaching a peak. The entire outer surface of the walls is covered with mesmerizing carvings of writhing feathered serpents coiling around the cross-legged "Lords of Time" priests.

Priests sit inside the Plumed Serpent's undulating coils on Xochicalco's pyramid.
Arian Zwegers from Brussels, Belgium, CC BY 2.0 <https://creativecommons.org/licenses/by/2.0>, via Wikimedia Commons; https://commons.wikimedia.org/wiki/File:Xochicalco,_Temple_of_the_Feathered_Serpent,_Maya_ruler_(20498593528).jpg

The hilltop city was an architectural masterpiece with retaining walls and terraces creating platforms linked by staircases and ramps. Defensive walls encircled the lower residential area, while the middle level featured a marketplace, ballcourt, palace, and elite residences. At the top of the hill were temples, pyramids, another ballcourt, and a large rainwater cistern. Raiders sacked and burned Xochicalco around 900 CE despite its formidable defense system. Three centuries later, the Tlahuica-Aztecs resettled the city as a lucrative cotton-growing and paper-producing center.

Uxmal

Uxmal (meaning "built three times") was another Maya Yucatán city in the Puuc ("hill") region about one hundred miles west of its sister city,

Chichén Itza. It was built in 500 CE by the long-lived Xiu dynasty and was the western Yucatán's most powerful city by 850, which was when most of its monumental buildings were erected. Conflict with the Toltecs who migrated to the region, compounded by the great drought, resulted in Uxmal's decline around 1100. The Xiu dynasty relocated to Maní, about twenty-five miles east.

The Maya built Uxmal to align with the rising and setting of Venus on auspicious calendar dates. Like Xochicalco, the city's architects had to contend with hilly terrain. The main ceremonial buildings had two stories. The first layer was punctuated by doorways with sculptures of the rain god Chaac over them. Lavish carvings and stone mosaics covered the second layer, with more images of Chaac at the corners.

Uxmal's ceremonial center has survived in good condition for over a millennium thanks to its expertly cut stones mortared with concrete. Uxmal's Pyramid of the Magician has rounded sides rather than sharp corners and was probably the earliest ceremonial building, built around 500 CE and expanded through the years. How did it get its name? One legend says that the magician god Itzamná erected it in one night. Another story is that a dwarf who hatched from an egg built the pyramid overnight through his mother's sorcery and became Uxmal's new king.

Tulum

Tulum sits on a bluff overlooking the Caribbean Sea in today's state of Quintana Roo. It was the last city built by the Yucatán Maya, with the surviving buildings constructed between 1200 and 1400 CE, although one stela and Building Fifty-nine date to the Classic era. Building Fifty-nine, the Temple of Nauyaca, is a modest one-story shrine outside the city's walls and close to the shore. It might have served as the ceremonial center for villages in the region before the city's construction.

The people of Tulum worshiped Ah Muzen Cab, the descending or diving god (or the bee god). Its image is carved into many of the city's ceremonial buildings. Tulum's seaside location made it a powerful contender in sea trade, especially with obsidian. Towering forty feet above the sea, this was one of the cities that astonished the early Spanish explorers who had not yet seen large buildings and complex cities in the New World.

El Castillo in Tulum.
Amber Funderburk Vyn, CC BY-SA 4.0 <https://creativecommons.org/licenses/by-sa/4.0>, via Wikimedia Commons; https://commons.wikimedia.org/wiki/File:CastilloTulum.jpg

The parts of Tulum not protected by the sheer cliffs dropping to the sea were encircled by a twelve-foot-high, two-foot-thick defensive wall with watchtowers on the western corners. A cenote sinkhole provided drinking water. The El Castillo structure served as a temple to the Feathered Serpent, with carvings of the deity adorning the lintels. It also served as a navigational guide to incoming canoes at its busy trade port, marking a break in the reef and a spot where a gentle slope led up to the city between the steep cliffs. Small fires in the windows on the side facing the sea lit the way for maritime traders arriving by night.

Key Takeaways:

- Ek' Balam
    - Long-lived Maya city near the top of the Yucatán Peninsula; capital of Talol Kingdom
    - Known for exquisite stucco relief carvings (including winged warriors) on a tomb

- Teotihuacan
    - Political empire over Valley of Mexico; trade empire extending to Central America
    - Human sacrifice at the state level from 150 to 350 CE
- Chichén Itza
    - Multicultural population and vast trade empire
    - Engaged in a long war against Spaniards
- Xochicalco
    - A blend of Maya and Teotihuacan architectural influence on the hilltop city
    - Fell to raiders around 900 CE, resettled in 1200 by Aztecs
- Uxmal
    - Built and ruled by the Xiu dynasty; it declined after Toltecs' arrival
    - Legend says the rounded Pyramid of the Magician was built in one night
- Tulum
    - Last city built by Yucatán Maya (between 1200 and 1400 CE)
    - Seaside trade center, with the El Castillo temple serving as a navigational guide

Chapter 15: Ancient Mythology and Cosmology

How did ancient Mexico's mythology and cosmology impact its history, art, and architecture? This chapter will explore the Mesoamerican understanding of the nature of the universe and how that influenced their belief system. The people of ancient Mexico believed the gods and other supernatural beings were intertwined with their everyday lives. Let's explore their myths, what their emblems revealed about their cosmology, some important rituals, and their understanding of the stars, planets, and eclipses.

Ancient Mexicans believed in mythological creatures that lived alongside humans and could bring good or evil their way. For example, the Yucatán Maya believed in leprechaun-like sprites called Aluxo'ob. They were usually invisible, but if people saw them, they looked like miniature Maya people about the size of a four-year-old child and wearing a loincloth. If the Maya heard weird noises at night, especially if they had just bought new land or were living in a new house, they said it was an Alux who was disturbed by the changes. The Maya also believed the Aluxo'ob could cause fevers and other health problems.

However, the Maya thought the Aluxo'ob mainly benefited humans because they helped people live in harmony with nature. The creator god, Junab K'uj, gave humans the stewardship of nature as their responsibility. After death, people could only make their way to heaven from the underworld if they had a proper relationship with nature in their lifetime.

The Aluxo'ob protected the fields and also lived in the jungles and caves.

When people respected the Aluxo'ob and gave them offerings, the sprites protected them. If a farmer built a little house in his fields, an Alux would move in and look after his land. It chased off animals or humans that would steal the crops and ensured plentiful rainfall. But at the end of seven years, the Alux would go berserk, causing all sorts of mischief, so the farmer had to seal it inside the little house.

The people of Chiapas believed that gigantic jaguar-like monsters with long, white beards called the Dzulum preyed on women, so they depended on the Balam to protect them. The Balam were shapeshifting, black panthers that guarded the four points of a village. Although magical, the Balam were mortal, as were the Dzulum. Monkeys were also useful in driving off the Dzulum monsters, as they would howl and harass the creatures until they left.

Nahual (or nagual) were humans with the unique ability to shapeshift, although they could only turn into one other animal, not multiple types of creatures. The Mesoamericans believed each person had a "tonal" animal intricately connected to them that could give them special powers (good and evil) and insight into spiritual things. People needed special training to learn how to shapeshift and usually used "magic mushrooms" or other hallucinogens to unlock their powers.

According to the Florentine Codex, the Aztecs believed the atotolin, the white pelican, ruled the rest of the birds. If a person tried to kill a white pelican, it would float in the middle of the lake, giving the person four days to try to shoot it. At sunset on the fourth day, the pelican would cry out, calling the wind, and the water would foam up as all the pelicans squawked and beat their wings. The human's arms froze, so he could not pole his boat, and the water would suck him in, drowning him. If a person managed to shoot a white pelican in the first four days, he would cut open the bird's gut and inspect the gizzard. If the hunter found a jade stone or precious feathers, it meant he would have good fortune, but if he found a piece of charcoal, it meant he would die.

In Aztec mythology, Cipactli was a primordial sea demon, something like a crocodile with multiple mouths, but it was also part fish and part toad. The myth of Cipactli preceded the Aztecs, as the Maya and Olmecs also believed in a crocodilian deity. The gods who created Cipactli realized it would devour the rest of creation with its insatiable appetite, so Tezcatlipoca and Quetzalcoatl caught it, although it ate Tezcatlipoca's foot. They hacked the creature to pieces, forming the heavens from its head, the earth from its midsection, and the underworld from its tail.

Quetzalcoatl and Tezcatlipoca from the Codex Borbonicus.
https://commons.wikimedia.org/wiki/File:Quetzalcoatl_and_Tezcatlipoca.jpg

The Aztecs and most ancient Mesoamericans believed that the world lay in utter darkness in the beginning and was covered by water. The god and goddess Tonacatecuhtli (Sky Father) and Tonacacihuatl (Earth Mother), who held first place in the calendar, created everything else: the stars, mountains, animals, and the other gods. But their first try at creating the earth failed, as the sun was too weak, so the god Tezcatlipoca became the sun. But his brother Quetzalcoatl got jealous and knocked him out of the sky, ending the first world.

In the second creation, Quetzalcoatl was the sun, but Tezcatlipoca got his revenge by blowing all the people off the earth and Quetzalcoatl out of the sky. The third time around, Tlaloc, the rain god, became the sun, but Quetzalcoatl got jealous again and burned up the earth and the sun. The surviving humans became turkeys. Tlaloc's wife, Chalchiuhtlicue, reigned as the sun in the fourth world. Unfortunately, all she knew how to do was make rain, so she drowned all the turkeys and covered the world with a great flood. Even the mountains were underwater.

The gods gathered at Teotihuacan, which the Aztecs believed was where the gods were born. Jealousy and foolishness had destroyed the first four ages: earth, wind, fire, and water. Quetzalcoatl and Tezcatlipoca were ashamed of how they had ruined the world multiple times and promised not to mess things up in the fifth world. They pushed the sky back up, separating it from the earth below. As the gods sat around a great bonfire, they decided that one of them would have to jump into the bonfire to become the next sun. The handsome god Tecciztecatl volunteered but couldn't work up the nerve to jump into the fire. He tried four times but stopped at the last minute.

The smallest and ugliest god, Nanahuatl, looked on in exasperation. He suddenly ran forward and jumped into the flames. After a few minutes, a bright light lit up the sky. It was Nanahuatl, now Tonatiuh, the sun of the fifth world. Tecciztecatl was disgusted with himself for letting the humble god Nanahuatl outshine him. He leaped into the fire, and everyone looked up to see two suns. One of the gods thought this was improper, so he lobbed a rabbit up at Tecciztecatl, dimming his light so that he became the moon with the image of a rabbit on it.

The Codex Chimalpopoca tells of the great flood that covered the mountains in the fourth world when Chalchiuhtlicue was making so much rain. Before it happened, the god Tezcatlipoca warned a man and his wife, Nata (or Tata) and Nena, to hollow out a giant cypress log and go inside it when the waters began to rise. He told them to take some ears of corn but not to eat anything else. But when the waters receded, there were fish everywhere, which Nata and Nena roasted and ate. When Tezcatlipoca smelled the smoke, he came down to see them eating the fish after he told them only to eat corn. He turned the couple into two dogs.

Once the gods successfully began the fifth world with the new sun and moon, they needed to recreate humans. Quetzalcoatl set off to Mictlán, the Aztec underworld, to bring back some of the bones of the earlier humans, many of whom had died because of his diabolical jealousy. The Aztecs considered bones the equivalent of seeds, which meant they could grow new people. He went with his brother Xolotl, the evening star, who knew the way to Mictlán, while Quetzalcoatl, the morning star, knew the way back.

The brothers cautiously approached Mictlantecuhtli, the Lord of the Dead, sitting on his throne surrounded by bones, spiders, and owls. Quetzalcoatl politely asked for some bones, but Mictlantecuhtli was unwilling until Quetzalcoatl explained that he was only borrowing them. Since humans were mortal, the bones would return to the underworld when the people died. The Lord of Death appeared to give permission, but on the way out, Quetzalcoatl fell into a pit that the devious Mictlantecuhtli had prepared to trap him. The bones shattered, but Quetzalcoatl quickly scooped them back into his bag and raced out. He and the other gods stabbed themselves and sprinkled their blood on the bones in penance for their sins that had destroyed the previous worlds. The bones were resurrected, but because they were broken, the new humans came in all shapes and sizes.

A replica of the Sun Stone painted in its original colors.
en:User:Ancheta Wis, CC BY-SA 2.5 <https://creativecommons.org/licenses/by-sa/2.5>, via Wikimedia Commons; https://commons.wikimedia.org/wiki/File:Aztec_Sun_Stone_Replica_cropped.jpg

The various civilizations of ancient Mexico had key emblems that represented their concept of cosmology. One example is the Aztec Sun Stone, a twelve-foot-wide circular stone with carvings depicting the Mexica-Aztec cosmology. Sometimes called the Calendar Stone, it has rays like the sun radiating out with a gruesome face with a protruding tongue in the center. Instead of hands, the creature has claws on each side. Although scholars debate who he is, most believe it is the sun god Tonatiuh. The disk represents the Aztec concept of the origin of the cosmos: the five "suns" or eras of the world before the gods finally succeeded. Tonatiuh, the sun of the fifth world, is in the center of the disk, surrounded by four images representing the four earlier worlds.

One implication of the Sun Stone is that the gods Tonatiuh and Tecciztecatl willingly sacrificed themselves to become the sun and the moon. Thus, humans should voluntarily feed the gods by sacrificing themselves. Around Tonatiuh's face and the symbols representing the previous worlds is a band of glyphs representing the twenty days in one month of the Aztec calendar. At the bottom of the disk are two fire serpents facing each other, representing time.

The Maya worshiped many of the same gods (with different names) that the Teotihuacanos, Toltecs, Aztecs, and other civilizations worshiped. They also believed in animism, the concept that animals, plants, and even inanimate things like rocks had a spirit. Thus, everything in nature was sacred to them. The Maya believed the world was a flat square and that four gods on each corner watched over the earth and protected it.

The thirteen layers of heaven were above the earth, and under the earth was Xibalba, nine layers of cold and unhappiness. Dead people had to work their way up through each layer before reaching the heavens. However, women who died in childbirth or people who were human sacrifices went straight to heaven. Everyone else had to follow the roots of the sacred Tree of Life up to its branches that spread out in the heavens. The gods also used the Tree of Life to travel from the heavens to earth and the underworld and back again, representing life's unending cycle.

The Aztecs had a similar concept of the heavens and the underworld, but they believed warriors killed in battle went straight to the eastern paradise, where they rested and recuperated for four years. After that, they were reincarnated as butterflies, eagles, hummingbirds, or owls. They believed that disabled people, lepers, people struck by lightning, and people who drowned went straight to the lowest level of heaven. This might have eased their consciences when they drowned babies as sacrifices to Tlaloc.

Elaborately costumed Maya priests perform rituals in this Bonampak fresco.
Photo zoomed in. Credit: Gary Todd from Xinzheng, China, CC0, via Wikimedia Commons; https://commons.wikimedia.org/wiki/File:Maya_Temple_of_the_Frescoes,_Bonampak,_Murals_C opied_by_Artist_Rina_Lazo_(9758814221).jpg

The priests dressed in elaborate costumes at religious festivals every twenty days in the sacred calendar of the Maya and other Mesoamericans. Paintings of the festival costumes can be seen in the art of Teotihuacan, in the Mixtec codices, and in the artwork of the Maya, Aztecs, and other groups. Once they were attired in their headdresses, masks, and clothing decorated with feathers, shells, and body plates, their appearance transformed into deities, animals, or famous historical people. They acted out symbolic plays, illustrating the cosmology associated with the festival.

Every twenty years, the Maya observed the K'atun ceremony of inscribing the events of the past two decades, such as the kings and wars, on a stone pillar or slab (stela). This ritual has provided invaluable information that gives us a glimpse into Maya history from centuries ago. Another Maya ritual involved mirrors, which they believed were a portal to the underworld. The especially daring Maya used mirrors to communicate with demons, a risky practice that, according to them, might have ended with them being snatched into the underworld.

The Maya and other Mesoamericans carefully observed the night sky, recording lunar and solar eclipses and the movement of Venus. The Toltecs connected the feathered serpent deity Quetzalcoatl with Venus, and the Mixtecs associated him with Mercury. The Mixtecs associated their flower and crocodile goddesses with eclipses but also connected the crocodile goddess with the moon, as the Maya and Aztecs did. Their understanding of astrology and astronomy guided their decisions and lifestyles.

Key Takeaways:
- Supernatural creatures
    - Aluxo'ob: sprites that helped preserve the balance of nature but could be mischievous
    - Dzulum: bearded jaguar monster; the Balam (panther) and monkeys guarded against them
    - Nahual: humans who could shapeshift into their spirit animal
    - Atotolin: white pelicans; hunters used their gizzards for divination
    - Cipactli: primordial crocodile-like sea demon who threatened to consume everything
- Creation myth
    - World originally in darkness covered by water
    - Gods destroyed the first four suns by jealousy and infighting
    - A humble god jumped into a bonfire, creating the fifth world (today's world)
    - Quetzalcoatl brought bones back from the underworld to make new humans
- Flood myth in Codex Chimalpopoca
    - The flood covered mountains, but Tezcatlipoca warned a man and woman to save themselves in a log
    - They disobeyed him and ate fish, so he turned them into dogs
- Aztec Sun Stone: represented the creation of the first five worlds and time
- Layers of heaven and underworld with the Tree of Life connecting them to earth
- Religious festivals every twenty days; costumed priests acted out cosmological beliefs
- Astronomy and astrology were important as gods were associated with stars and eclipses

Chapter 16: Ancient Mexican Culture and Legacy

Ancient Mexico's culture was a rich array of art, architecture, written language, and religious beliefs. While each civilization had unique contributions, they all shared certain cultural aspects. These shared customs and values flowed from a legacy chain beginning with the Olmecs and other older cultures, subsequently impacting later cultures. Robust trade relations between civilizations led to an interchange of architecture, art, and religion.

How are art and architecture linked to cultural development? In ancient Mexico, art expressed the people's cosmology and understanding of the supernatural. Architecture conveyed religious and political themes, and art and architecture tracked historical events and cultural perspectives. In cities like Teotihuacan, with virtually no literary history, we rely on its art and architecture as a glimpse into its society, politics, religious beliefs, and the changes that shook the city. Even with a written history, such as the Mixtecs or Aztecs, art gives us a deeper understanding of what life was like for ordinary people, not just rulers, priests, and warriors.

Art and architecture can also be used as propaganda to mold public opinion and initiate social, political, and religious change. For instance, we never see artistic depictions of people bowing to their kings in Teotihuacan. The Teotihuacanos didn't glorify their rulers through art. They did paint murals and carved images of their deities, and we see numerous examples of priests offering sacrifices to the gods. But most paintings of warriors or ordinary people show little distinction, almost like repetitive images on wallpaper.

Teotihuacan architecture also seemed to broadcast a message. The city had massive pyramids of several gods in its center, but most of the metropolis consisted of over two thousand apartment complexes, relatively equal in design. From this, archaeologists glean that, for at least part of its history, Teotihuacan promoted a collective society led by a council rather than a hierarchal system ruled by a king. Equality between individuals was promoted in Teotihuacan's art and architecture.

The Aztecs also used architecture for political and religious propaganda. As they conquered new territories, spreading their empire from the Pacific Ocean to the Gulf Coast, they permitted their new subjects to continue worshiping their traditional deities. However, they had to honor the Aztec chief deity, Huitzilopochtli, as the highest deity. To emphasize this, the Aztecs built majestic temples to Huitzilopochtli, god of the sun and war, on mountaintops and in the city centers of their new territories.

Additionally, the Aztecs used art and architecture in their capital of Tenochtitlan to promote the worship of Huitzilopochtli and tell his story. The highest pyramid in Tenochtitlan was the Templo Mayor, which symbolized Mount Coatepec, the hill in the middle of their ancestral island of Aztlán. According to Aztec myth, when Huitzilopochtli's siblings discovered their mother was pregnant with him, his four hundred brothers, led by his sister Coyolxauhqui, attacked her.

Huitzilopochtli spurted out of his mother's belly, fully grown, and sliced his sister's head off. Her body tumbled to the bottom of the hill, breaking into pieces, while Huitzilopochtli killed his brothers and ate their hearts. In 1978, a massive stone was uncovered at the foot of the Templo Mayor's stairs, which depicted Coyolxauhqui with her head and limbs severed from her body. Over ten feet in diameter, the stone's location at the bottom of the model of Mount Coatepec symbolized the story of her gruesome end at the hands of her brother.

Coyolxauhqui's dismembered body on a replica of the Templo Mayor stone.
*Photograph by Mike Peel (www.mikepeel.net)., CC BY-SA 4.0
<https://creativecommons.org/licenses/by-sa/4.0>, via Wikimedia Commons;
https://commons.wikimedia.org/wiki/File:Templo_Mayor_2015_007.jpg*

The civilizations of ancient Mexico didn't arise and develop in a vacuum. They inherited a rich legacy from the cultures that preceded them, and even the oldest complex civilizations interacted with other cultures. This legacy chain began in places like the Guilá Naquitz Cave near Mitla in the Oaxaca Valley, where sophisticated agriculture began in Mexico around 6000 BCE. The cave contained seeds for squash, corn, and beans, which comprised the Three Sisters planting system that spread throughout Mexico and the rest of North America.

Ceramics emerged in ancient Mexico about three hundred miles west of Mitla at Puerto Marqués and La Zanja in Guerrero, possibly dating as early as 2400 BCE. The Mokaya people of Paso de la Amada in the state of Chiapas were the first to build large-scale architecture, including Mexico's first-known ballcourt around 1650 BCE. The ballcourt became an essential feature in most other prominent cultures of ancient Mexico.

The Olmecs began using the 260-day ceremonial calendar by 800 BCE, which the rest of ancient Mexico's advanced civilizations adopted. The earliest known writings in Mexico were simple glyphs carved into the Cascajal Block by the Olmecs in the 10th century BCE. The Maya began using pictorial glyphs about 900 BCE. The Zapotecs of Monte Albán developed hieroglyphics in the logo-syllabic system around 500 BCE, and the Maya started using sophisticated hieroglyphics by 300.

By then, the Epi-Olmecs had developed the Isthmian script as seen on a pottery shard in Chiapa de Corzo on the Pacific coast. Although the Isthmian script had structural similarities to Mayan and Zapotec hieroglyphics, all three writing systems developed independently. They all used pictorial symbols or logograms for nouns and some verbs, and they used phonetic symbols for sounds, but each culture wrote the symbols differently.

Intriguingly, this literary legacy did not spread to other ancient Mexican civilizations as quickly as would be expected. Teotihuacan and the Toltec capital of Tula only show evidence of simple glyphs, despite being influential cities with copious interactions with the literate Maya and Zapotecs. The Mixtecs adopted the logographic system used by the Zapotecs in the Postclassic era, and the Aztecs also copied a variant of the Zapotec script.

The Maya left stunning contributions in art and architecture to the legacy chain passed down to other cultures in Mexico. Some Maya innovations in architecture included extraordinarily steep and high pyramids, pyramids with rounded sides, multi-story buildings, the corbelled arch, and corbelled roofing. A distinguishing feature of Maya architecture is that non-religious buildings were often as ornate as temples. The Maya loved to cover the exterior of buildings with intricate carvings and relief work.

Murals were a favorite of the Maya, a love they adopted from the Olmecs. In Calakmul, at the base of the Yucatán, they had a painted pyramid covered with panels of murals dating to around 600 to 700 CE.

The vivid paintings showed ordinary people rather than the usual kings, priests, or warriors. About one-third of the images were of women, who were rarely depicted in Maya or other Mesoamerican art. Hieroglyphics next to the murals served as captions explaining some of the scenes: preparing corn porridge, offering tamales to eat, and spooning tobacco from a jar. They provide a vivid picture of how non-elite Maya went about their days and what they wore and consumed.

Calakmul's painted pyramid shows maize brew being prepared and served.
Bernard DUPONT, CC BY-SA 2.0 <https://creativecommons.org/licenses/by-sa/2.0>, via Wikimedia Commons;
https://commons.wikimedia.org/wiki/File:Reproduction_of_Mural_from_Structure_I,_Calakmul.jpg

While the Maya innovated, the Mexica-Aztecs assimilated. As the newcomers to central Mexico, they arrived after wandering the northwestern deserts for decades. They paused in Tula for twenty years to absorb the majestic culture of the nearly abandoned Toltec city. They passed through the ghost town of Teotihuacan, which was even more breathtaking than Tula. They also wandered around the Lake Texcoco system and hired themselves out as workers and soldiers to the other tribes in the area, gathering more cultural information. When they settled Tenochtitlan and established their empire, they imported Mixtec goldsmiths and scribes, the latter of whom wrote the codices that filled their libraries.

The Mexica-Aztecs assimilated Quetzalcoatl, Tlaloc, and other deities from the tribes around them, but they clung to their hummingbird god Huitzilopochtli. They adopted Toltec art and sculptures like the chacmool and the serpent wall in Tula. They learned writing from the Mixtecs and adopted the Mesoamerican calendar. They studied Teotihuacan's architecture and traveled there to offer sacrifices.

Ancient Mexico had several primary language families. Mayan was the language family of the independent Maya city-states scattered throughout southern Mexico and Central America. The Zapotecs, Mixtecs, and Otomi spoke the Otomanguean languages. The people of Veracruz, Puebla, and Hidalgo spoke the Totonacan languages. Nahuatl was the language of the Aztec tribes, the Chichimeca, and probably the Toltecs.

Teotihuacan was a multilingual city, with the Otomanguean languages, Mayan, and Totonacan languages all being spoken. Teotihuacan probably used a northern variant of the Otomanguean language as its dominant administrative language. In the late Classic era, as the Chichimeca tribes migrated south, they brought the Nahuatl language with them. Nahuatl soon became the lingua franca (common language) of the Valley of Mexico.

How did religious belief develop in ancient Mexico? Some scholars believe that central and southern Mexico had one religion expressed in several ways by the Olmecs, Maya, Teotihuacanos, and Zapotecs. This core cosmology was passed on to the Mixtecs, Toltecs, and Aztecs. Other scholars argue that each major civilization had a different belief system yet exchanged ideas with other cultures and developed a syncretism or blend of beliefs.

Clearly, the primary cultures of ancient Mexico shared common religious ideas. They all followed the 260-day sacred calendar and believed the world was originally covered by water and darkness before the present age. They all worshiped the feathered serpent deity and believed he was involved in creation. They also all worshiped the rain deity as a primary god and sacrificed children to him. They all practiced human sacrifice, but the Toltecs and Aztecs remembered a time when they did not sacrifice humans. They believed that people went to one of heaven's levels or to the underworld when they died.

The 260-day sacred calendar, human sacrifice, the Feathered Serpent, and the rain deity all track back to the Olmecs. However, the Olmec rain god was a were-jaguar, not the goggle-eyed fanged creature worshiped by the later cultures of ancient Mexico. The Maya rain god Chaac did not always have goggle eyes, but he did have fangs. He had a human-like body with reptilian scales and a drooping nose that covered his mouth.

Chaak, the Maya rain god.
Gary Todd, CC0, via Wikimedia Commons;
https://commons.wikimedia.org/wiki/File:Chaak_Vessel,_Mayapan,_Post_Classic,_1250-1450_AD.jpg

Despite not having pack animals and sailing technology, long-distance trade flourished in ancient Mexico. In the Classic era, Teotihuacan was a massive market hub with trade networks extending from the Pacific to the Gulf Coast and deep into Central America. Their most vital trade partners were the Maya. Teotihuacan had a near-monopoly on the obsidian trade, which they exchanged for luxury goods, such as exotic feathers, chocolate, and jade.

Hundreds of years later, the Aztecs of Tenochtitlan controlled most of the trade within central and southern Mexico. The *pochteca*, or merchants, even had a god of commerce called Yacatecuhtli. The robust trade networks of ancient Mexico carried technical information, such as farming techniques and metalworking. Religious ideas were shared, and innovative ideas about art and architecture spread. Flourishing trade indelibly impacted ancient Mexico's legacy chain of culture and technology.

Key Takeaways:
- How are art and architecture linked to cultural development?
    - Art and architecture give a glimpse into cultural development within cultures.

- o Art and architecture can be used as propaganda to promote cultural change or impose political and religious ideology.
- A legacy chain of the older and later cultures of ancient Mexico
  - o Sophisticated agriculture, ceramics, and ballcourt developed in western Mexico
  - o Olmecs and Maya used first simple glyphs
  - o Zapotecs used the first sophisticated hieroglyphics, followed by Maya and Epi-Olmecs
  - o Mixtecs and Aztecs adopted the Zapotec writing system
- Factors that influenced the legacy chain or were influenced by it
  - o Maya legacy of art and architecture; Aztec assimilation of multiple cultures
  - o Language development and adoption of different languages
  - o Developments in religious belief
  - o The impact of trade relations between civilizations

Conclusion

The legacies of ancient Mexico endured through the colonial era and continue to shape modern-day Mexico. If not for its ancient civilizations, would Mexico be the nation it is today? Would our world be the same?

The Olmecs introduced many "firsts" to Mexico and the world. By 1700 BCE, the Olmecs were roasting cacao beans to make a chocolate drink, which became wildly popular among the elite in Mexico. The Spaniards introduced chocolate to Europe in the early 1500s, and soon, shipments of cacao beans were traveling from Veracruz to Spain, where hot cocoa became a court delicacy. Today, people consume 7.5 million tons of chocolate products worldwide.

The Olmecs and Maya began using simple pictorial glyphs around 900 BCE, and by 500 BCE, the Zapotecs developed complex hieroglyphics with symbols for nouns and sounds. The Maya, Epi-Olmecs, Mixtecs, and Aztecs subsequently developed written languages. This literacy meant a sizable portion of ancient Mexico's history was preserved.

The Franciscan friars thought the indigenous people would be more open to Christianity if they introduced it in their languages. The friars learned Nahuatl, converted it to the Latin alphabet, then taught the young men to read their language with the alphabet. The Franciscan friars interviewed the indigenous people about their culture and history and read their codices. Fray Bernardino de Sahagún translated the Gospels and the Psalms into Nahuatl and recorded the Aztec culture and history in the Florentine Codex. Fray Diego Durán wrote the Durán Codex or the *Historia de las Indias de Nueva España* in 1581, translating from the

Aztec documents.

The Dominican friars challenged Sahagún and Durán, considering all aspects of the indigenous peoples' culture evil, including their language. The Dominicans destroyed priceless codices and artifacts to impose Spanish culture. But some of Mexico's ancient history was preserved thanks to the Franciscans. The ancient languages survived, with 1.5 million people speaking Nahuatl today and 4.5 million Mexicans speaking other indigenous languages.

Both the Franciscans and Dominicans were pleased when the indigenous people quickly agreed to be baptized as Catholics. They didn't realize that most simply added the Virgin Mary and Jesus to their polytheistic system. The Aztecs had imposed the worship of Huitzilopochtli on the conquered people of Mexico while allowing them to keep their own gods. They were used to this system and merely added Catholicism into the mix. However, they did discard Huitzilopochtli altogether, along with human sacrifice.

Some of the religious practices of ancient Mexico have continued up to the present day in a syncretistic blend with Catholic Christianity. For instance, the Aztec descendants in northern Veracruz worship Ometotiotsij, the ancient Aztec god Ometeotl. Also known as the Sky Father Tonacatecuhtli, he and his wife Tonacacihuatl (Earth Mother) created the universe and the rest of the gods in ancient Mexican cosmology.

The Day of the Dead, celebrated throughout today's Mexico, originated in an Aztec festival celebrating Mictlantecuhtli and Mictecacihuatl, Lord and Lady of the Underworld. Some indigenous people in the Puebla region worship the "Solar Christ," whom they associate with the sun god Tonatiuh. Many Mexicans believe the ancient Aztec mother earth goddess Tonantzin is Our Lady of Guadalupe (the Virgin Mary). The Basilica of Guadalupe was built over a temple to Tonantzin in today's Mexico City.

While inventing chocolate, the Olmecs also mixed sap from the rubber tree and morning glory vines to make rubber balls. This invention led to the game of ulama, which quickly impacted the rest of central and southern Mexico, where over two thousand ancient ballcourts have been unearthed. Ulama is still played today in Sinaloa, Mexico, making it the longest continuously played sport in history. When the Spaniards showed up three thousand years later, they were delighted by the rubber balls and the ulama game. Cortés sent a ball team with bouncy balls to perform for King Charles in 1528.

Over the centuries, the Europeans experimented with rubber, forming erasers in 1770, rubber raincoats in 1824, and shoe soles and bicycle tires in the 1880s. In 1856, Charles Goodyear invented soccer balls made from vulcanized rubber. Before this, teams used pig bladders to play a prototype of soccer (football), similar to the Mexican ulama game. The main difference was that the ball could touch the ground and be kicked with the feet. In ulama, the players hit the ball with their heads, elbows, legs, and hips to keep it in the air and in play. Today, football (or soccer in the US) is Mexico's number one sport and the most popular game globally, thanks to the Olmecs and their bouncy balls.

Many of the Spanish colonists of Mexico were single men, or they left their wives behind. They took indigenous women as their wives or mistresses, who gave birth to *mestizo* children. In today's Mexico, 93 percent of the population are at least partially descended from the ancient people of Mexico, and 15 percent are fully indigenous. The legacy of ancient Mexico lives on through its people.

Here's another book by Enthralling History that you might like

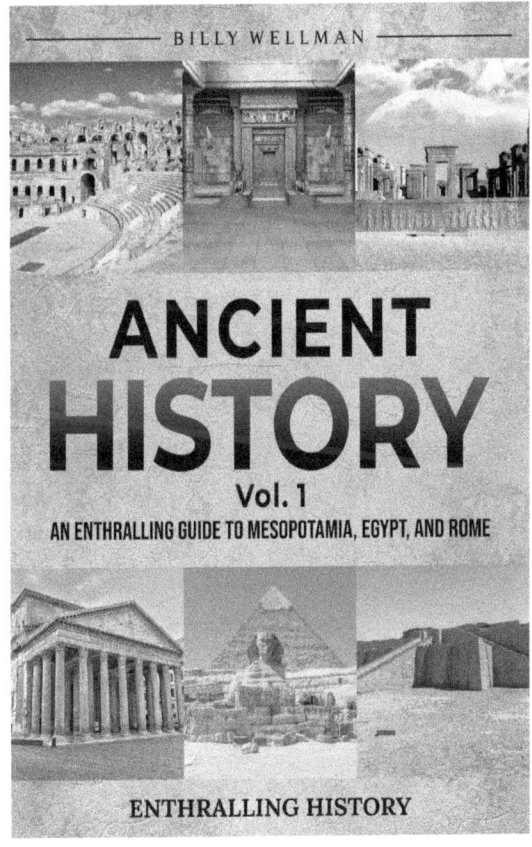

Free limited time bonus

Stop for a moment. We have a free bonus set up for you. The problem is this: we forget 90% of everything that we read after 7 days. Crazy fact, right? Here's the solution: we've created a printable, 1-page pdf summary for this book that you're reading now. All you have to do to get your free pdf summary is to go to the following website:

https://livetolearn.lpages.co/enthrallinghistory/

Once you do, it will be intuitive. Enjoy, and thank you!

Bibliography

Blomster, J.P., and Chávez Salazar. "Origins of the Mesoamerican Ballgame: Earliest Ballcourt from the Highlands Found at Etlatongo, Oaxaca, Mexico." *Science Advances* 6, no. 11 (March 13, 2020). doi: 10.1126/sciadv.aay6964. PMID: 32201726; PMCID: PMC7069692.

Carballo, David M. *Urbanization and Religion in Ancient Central Mexico*. New York: Oxford University Press, 2016.

Carter, Robert F. "North America's First Shipyard." *The Military Engineer* 57, no. 379 (1965): 338-40. http://www.jstor.org/stable/44571688.

Coe, Michael D., Javier Urcid, Rex Koontz. *Mexico: From the Olmecs to the Aztecs*. New York: Thames & Hudson, September 17, 2019.

Coe, Michael D. *The Maya (Ancient Peoples and Places Series)*. London and New York: Thames & Hudson, 1999.

Cortés, Hernán. *Cartas y Relaciones de Hernán Cortés al Emperador Carlos V*. Edited by Pascual de Gayangos. Paris: A. Chaix, 1866. https://www.cervantesvirtual.com/nd/ark:/59851/bmc0974782

Cowgill, George L. *Ancient Teotihuacan: Early Urbanism in Central Mexico (Case Studies in Early Societies)*. Cambridge: Cambridge University Press, 2015.

Cowgill, George L. "State and Society at Teotihuacan, Mexico." *Annual Review of Anthropology* 26 (1997): 129-61. http://www.jstor.org/stable/2952518.

Demarest, Arthur. *Ancient Maya: The Rise and Fall of a Forest Civilization*. Cambridge: Cambridge University Press, 2004. ISBN 978-0-521-53390-4. OCLC 51438896.

Díaz del Castillo, Bernal. *The Conquest of New Spain*. Translated by J. M. Cohen. Harmondsworth, England: Penguin Books, 1963 [1632].

Elzey, Wayne. "A Hill on a Land Surrounded by Water: An Aztec Story of Origin and Destiny." *History of Religions*, 31, no. 2 (1991):105-49. http://www.jstor.org/stable/1063021.

Evans, Susan T. *Ancient Mexico and Central America: Archaeology and Culture History*. London: Thames and Hudson, 2004.

Flannery, Kent V., and Joyce Marcus. "Las Sociedades Jerárquicas Oaxaqueñas y el Intercambio con los Olmecas." *Arqueología Mexicana*, 87, (2007): 71-76.

Frey, Georges. "The Endless Conquest of Yucatán." *Popular Archaeology*. January 14, 2022.

García-Des Lauriers, Claudia, ed. and Tatsuya Murakami, ed. Teotihuacan and Early Classic Mesoamerica: Multiscalar Perspectives on Power, Identity, and Interregional Relations. Louisville: University Press of Colorado, 2021.

Grennes-Ravitz, Ronald A., and G. H. Coleman. "The Quintessential Role of Olmec in the Central Highlands of Mexico: A Refutation." *American Antiquity* 41, no. 2 (1976): 196-206. https://doi.org/10.2307/279172.

Hassig, Ross. *Time, History, and Belief in Aztec and Colonial Mexico*. Austin: University of Texas Press, 2001.

Hassig, Ross. *War and Society in Ancient Mesoamerica*. Berkeley: University of California Press, 1992.

Headrick, Annabeth. *The Teotihuacan Trinity: The Sociopolitical Structure of an Ancient Mesoamerican City (The William and Bettye Nowlin Series in Art, History, and Culture of the Western Hemisphere)*. Austin: University of Texas Press, 2017.

Hipolito, Daniel Santos, and Jose Antonio Casanova Meneses. "Armas Mixtecas Acercan al Público al Arte de la Guerra entre los Mixtecos durante el Posclásico." *Instituto Nacional de Antropología e Historia* 36 (February 2018). https://inah.academia.edu/DanielSantosHipolito

History and Mythology of the Aztecs: The Codex Chimalpopoca. Translated by John Bierhorst. Tucson: The University of Arizona Press, 1992.

Hirth, Kenneth G., David M. Carballo, and Barbara Arroyo. *Teotihuacan: The World Beyond the City*. Washington, D.C.: Dumbarton Oaks, 2020.

Holt Mehta, Haley. *Colonial Encounters, Creolization, and the Classic Period Zapotec Diaspora: Questions of Identity from El Tesoro, Hidalgo, Mexico*. PhD diss., Tulane University, 2019.

Hosler, Dorothy, Sandra Burkett, and Michael Tarkanian. "Prehistoric Polymers: Rubber Processing in Ancient Mesoamerica." *Science*. June 18, 1999, 1988-91. doi:10.1126/science.284.5422.1988. OCLC 207960606. PMID 10373117.

Houston, Stephen, and David Stuart. Stuart, David. "Of Gods, Glyphs, and Kings: Divinity and Rulership among the Classic Maya." *Antiquity* 70, no. 268 (1996): 289-312. doi:10.1017/S0003598X00083289.

Inomata, T, D., F. Triadan, F. Pinzón, and K. Aoyama. "Artificial Plateau Construction during the Preclassic Period at the Maya Site of Ceibal, Guatemala." *PLoS One.* 2019 Aug 30;14(8):e0221943. doi: 10.1371/journal.pone.0221943. PMID: 31469887; PMCID: PMC6716660

Joyce, Arthur A. "Interregional Interaction and Social Development on the Oaxaca Coast." *Ancient Mesoamerica.* 4, no. 1 (1993): 67-84. http://www.jstor.org/stable/26307326.

Kennedy, Alison Bailey. "Ecce Bufo: The Toad in Nature and in Olmec Iconography." *Current Anthropology* 23, no. 3 (1982): 273-90. http://www.jstor.org/stable/2742313.

Manzanilla, Linda R. "Cooperation and Tensions in Multi-ethnic Corporate Societies Using Teotihuacan, Central Mexico, as a Case Study." *Proceedings of the National Academy of Sciences.* 112, no.30 (March 2015): 9210-15. https://doi.org/10.1073/pnas.1419881112

Matthew, Laura E., and Michel R. Oudijk. *Indian Conquistadors: Indigenous Allies in the Conquest of Mesoamerica.* University of Oklahoma Press, October 22, 2012.

McVicker, Donald. "The 'Mayanized' Mexicans." *American Antiquity* 50, no. 1 (1985): 82-101. https://doi.org/10.2307/280635.

Miller, Mary Ellen. *The Art of Mesoamerica: From Olmec to Aztec (World of Art).* Thames & Hudson, 2019.

Moran, Barbara. "Lessons from Teo." *The Brink: Boston University,* 2015. https://www.bu.edu/articles/2015/archaeology-teotihuacan-mexico/

Pasztory, Esther. *Teotihuacan: An Experiment in Living.* Norman: University of Oklahoma Press, 1997.

Pomar, Juan Bautista de. "Relación de Tezcoco," In *Relaciones de la Nueva España,* edited by Vázquez Chamorro. Madrid: Historia 16, 1991.

Powis T. G., A. Cyphers, N. W. Gaikwad, L. Grivetti, and K. Cheong. "Cacao Use and the San Lorenzo Olmec." *Proceedings of the National Academy of Sciences,* 108 (21) (2011): 8595-600, https://www.researchgate.net/publication/51110764_Cacao_Use_and_the_San_Lorenzo_Olmec

Pratt, John P. "Ixtlilxochitl's Toltec History," August 1, 2019, https://www.johnpratt.com/items/docs/2019/ixtlil.html

Recker, Jane. "Researchers Decipher the Glyphs on a 1,300-Year-Old Frieze in Mexico." *Smithsonian Magazine,* March 8, 2022.

https://www.smithsonianmag.com/smart-news/researchers-decipher-the-glyphs-on-a-1300-year-old-frieze-in-mexico-180979691/

Robb, Matthew, ed. *Teotihuacan: City of Water, City of Fire.* Berkeley: University of California Press, 2017.

Sabloff, Jeremy A. "It Depends on How We Look at Things: New Perspectives on the Postclassic Period in the Northern Maya Lowlands." *Proceedings of the American Philosophical Society* 151, no. 1 (2007): 11-26. http://www.jstor.org/stable/4599041

Sahagún, Fray Bernardino de. *Historia General de las Cosas de Nueva España.* Edited by Francisco del Paso y Troncoso. Madrid: Fototipia de Hauser y Menet, 1905.

Schroeder, Susan, ed. *Chimalpahin's Conquest: A Nahua Historian's Rewriting of Francisco Lopez de Gomara's La conquista de Mexico.* Redwood City: Stanford University Press, 2010. https://doi.org/10.1515/9780804775069-184

Shook, Edwin M., and Alfred V. Kidder. "Mound E-III-3, K'aminaljuyu, Guatemala." In *Contributions to American Anthropology and History*, Vol. 9 (53) (1952): 33-127. Washington DC: Carnegie Institution of Washington.

Smith, Michael E., Abhishek Chatterjee, Angela C. Huster, Sierra Stewart, and Marion Forest. "Apartment Compounds, Households, and Population in the Ancient City of Teotihuacan, Mexico." *Ancient Mesoamerica* 30, no. 3 (2019): 399-418. doi:10.1017/S0956536118000573.

Smith, Michael E., and Kenneth G. Hirth. "The Development of Prehispanic Cotton-Spinning Technology in Western Morelos, Mexico." *Journal of Field Archaeology* 15 (1988): 349-358.

Spence, Lewis. *The Myths of Mexico and Peru.* London: George Harrap, 1913. https://www.sacred-texts.com/nam/mmp/index.htm

Sprajc, Ivan, Takeshi Inomata, and Anthony F. Aveni. "Origins of Mesoamerican Astronomy and Calendar: Evidence from the Olmec and Maya Regions." *Science Advances* 9, no. 1 (2023). doi:10.1126/sciadv.abq7675.

Sugiyama, Nawa, Saburo Sugiyama, and Alejandro Sarabia. "Inside the Sun Pyramid at Teotihuacan, Mexico: 2008–2011 Excavations and Preliminary Results." *Latin American Antiquity* 24, no. 4 (2013): 403-32. http://www.jstor.org/stable/23645621.

Taube, Karl A. "The Teotihuacan Cave of Origin: The Iconography and Architecture of Emergence Mythology in Mesoamerica and the American Southwest." RES: *Anthropology and Aesthetics*, no. 12 (1986): 51-82. http://www.jstor.org/stable/20166753.

Townsend, Richard F. *The Aztecs* (3rd, revised ed.). London: Thames & Hudson, 2009.